If You Love Me, Take Me Now

If You Love Me, Take Me Now

BY
STEVE COX

Copyright © 2015 by Steve Cox

All rights reserved. No part of this book may be reproduced, scanned or distributed in any printed or electronic form without permission. Please do not participate or encourage piracy of copyrighted materials in violation of the author's rights. Purchase only authorized editions.

Cox, Steve
If You Love Me, Take Me Now

Designed by Phillip Gessert
Edited by The Threepenny Editor

Printed in the United States of America

10 9 8 7 6 5 4 3 2 1

This book is dedicated to the pursuit of a cure for brain cancer

The names of doctors have been changed for privacy purposes.

INTRODUCTION
BY DR. MARK GILBERT

The diagnosis of cancer has many ramifications for patients themselves, their family and friends. There have been many publications both in professional journals and the lay press that describe the various stages and emotions that people experience after receiving the news. For most, there is the expected dread, given the association of the cancer diagnosis with concerns regarding survival and the anticipation of the short and long-term side effects of treatment. Some patients, paradoxically, are relieved to know that there is a reason for their symptoms and that the possibility of treatment focused on the cause and hopefully relief leads to a sense of hope.

Almost universally, however, patients who are told that they have cancer experience uncertainty. This results from questions about prognosis, treatment options, and where to get treatment. These issues become paramount as patients tackle the immediate challenges that emerge soon after the diagnosis.

The memoir by Steve Cox that follows this Foreword very poignantly describes his journey with cancer. It is a very moving story, appropriately told from the first person, as it is Steve's personal journey. He is very articulate in describing all of the aspects of this arduous expedition from a "typical" middle class, family-oriented environment to the struggle with the devastation of a rare cancer.

Why should we be interested in this very personal account of a serious illness? His cancer is very rare so it is very, very unlikely that anyone reading this book (unless they read it because *they* have this type of cancer) would get this cancer or know anyone who does. The answer lies in the lessons that his and his family's experience teaches us about dealing with serious illness and in the important implications for tackling the cancer problem, now the number one killer in the United States.

From a personal standpoint, the memoir is a moving and captivating retelling of his experiences. He demonstrates tremendous inner strength motivated by his love and concern for his family. His revelations about his new life after the diagnosis and treatment inspired great respect and appreciation from me as well as insight into the journey that many of my patients must have experienced during their personal experiences with cancer.

There are additional aspects of this story that are important to consider. His diagnosis is of a rare cancer of the nervous system. This brings on extra challenges. He had difficulty finding healthcare providers with expertise so that he could be reassured that state-of-the-art care was being provided. Fortunately, the Internet now provides access to a wealth of information, but caution needs to be exercised as not all the information available is trustworthy. Rare cancers present additional challenges, as research activities are often limited both because of small patient populations and limited funding—allocation of research support typically mirrors the incidence of the disease.

I have been involved in brain tumor research for nearly 30 years and much of the narrative resonated with me at the personal level, having cared for many patients with brain cancer as well as at the professional level. Fortunately, brain tumors are relatively uncommon but as a consequence, there has been limited funding for research. Recently, there has been more resources allocated for the more common brain tumors, but the rare cancers truly remain "orphan" diseases.

Steve's diagnosis of ependymoma clearly places him in the rare cancer category. This is a cancer of the central nervous system that is very uncommon in adults and has traditionally been considered primarily a pediatric disease. Until recently, there were very few scholarly publications examining ependymoma in adults. My personal involvement with this disease begins with one of my patients that led philanthropic support and to the creation of the Collaborative Ependymoma Research Network (www.CERN-foundation.org) that has focused a major research effort in both adult and pediatric ependymomas. The investigations include clinical and laboratory science, evaluation of patient outcomes and a major effort in outreach, awareness and education. I describe CERN with great pride as it represents a model to tackle the problem of rare cancers. Through CERN, patients and their families can learn about the disease, find centers of excellence for consultation and care, and stay abreast of developments. Increasing awareness of the disease leads to a dissemination of knowledge and the potential for global improvement in treatments. In this context, clinical trials, previously deemed impractical can now be considered. It is through these efforts that treatments will lead to better outcomes.

This memoir offers much insight into the cancer journey and highlights the challenges and shortcomings of the current state of treatment. However, we should be heartened and encouraged by the generous support offered by many philanthropic and patient advocacy groups. By working together, we can make the cancer journey less daunting and provide hope of future advances.

Dr. Gilbert graduated from The Johns Hopkins University with a Bachelor's Degree in Biology in 1979 and went on to earn his Medical Degree in 1982. He completed his training at the Johns Hopkins Hospital under the leadership of Dr. Stuart (Skip) Grossman.

1

There was something about the way he looked at me. His face had gone pale and the expression on his face made him seem to want to say something to me. Instead the technician just stood at the doorway as I exited the MRI room at Parkland Hospital. For the past half an hour I had been snoozing in the MRI machine, or the tube as I came to know it. Except for the injection of gadolinium in my arm, and the earplug-muffled buzz inside the machine, the whole experience was relaxing.

The technician had been with me the whole time up till now, watching the image of my brain appearing on the monitor beyond the room's window. The MRI machine was in its own chamber and the machine controls were adjacent and behind glass. When I'd entered he hadn't even looked up when the nurse greeted me; but now, he held the door for me and looked somber. Maybe he was having a bad day, or maybe he knew my day was going to get much worse.

If You Love Me, Take Me Now

Odd things had been happening to me for several months. Looking back, I had been having symptoms for more than a year. Headaches would last for days. Tylenol or Advil made them tolerable, but I'd have to consume a steady diet of pills while they lasted. I figured my demanding job as a middle manager in a fast-paced tech firm was the cause. Then the hiccups started. At first I didn't think much of it, but they got worse. I'd hiccup daily. They became so frequent that every time I started eating or drinking I'd have to stop and wait for them to pass. I couldn't get through a meal without being disturbed. On other occasions, if I rolled over in bed while sleeping, I'd hiccup myself awake. They'd start in the middle of a conversation. They were a real nuisance, and were the first obvious sign that something was wrong.

I was married to the woman of my dreams. We had a son and daughter in college. For our first dozen years of marriage, we squeaked by paycheck to paycheck. The money came just in time to pay our bills. I was in middle management and Barbara worked in the local school system. We didn't focus on what we didn't have and life was good. As time passed, my career progressed to the point where we had more than we ever thought we would. Not great wealth by anyone's measure, but enough to have a little to save after the bills were paid. Life seemed to be getting better every day.

All my life, I had looked after my health. I worked in high-tech sales for a US company. My division was based in Vienna, Austria, and my travel routine was international and heavy. Despite this, my exercise regimen included jogging five miles daily. I was trim and in great shape. I had always practiced the healthcare theory that if you wait long enough, whatever is ailing you will go way.

But after a year of hiccups, I knew they weren't going away. In late August of 2003 I finally decided to see a doctor. He listened to my complaints and referred me to a gastroenterologist, a stomach doctor. It made sense to me. There must be something going on in my gut that was upsetting my diaphragm and causing hiccups. Yet because the stomach doctor had a busy practice, he was not able to see me until late October. Over the several weeks' wait, the symptoms worsened.

The stomach doctor started me on a prescription of antacids. His suspicion was that stomach acid was upsetting my diaphragm. "Come back and see me in a few weeks," he instructed. In the meantime, my job was keeping me busy with travel. In a few days I was off to China for a week. While there, the medication did not alleviate my symptoms. If anything, they got worse. One evening, in a nice restaurant at a company dinner, I sat at a large round table among the upper management of my employer's Chinese division. To my immediate right was the top man, the president of the division. A Chinese national. Of course, I was on my best behavior and careful not to make any blunders, cultural or otherwise, that might embarrass or insult my hosts. There was a large lazy-Susan stocked with various Chinese delights. Most Westerners usually do not find them very appetizing, myself included: crispy pig's ears, fried chicken feet, blood-curd soup, and other culinary delights. I "happily" dug in like the rest of my Chinese colleagues and pretended to enjoy the local cuisine. The whole time I was fighting off hiccups and resisting the nausea that came with every crunch of a chicken foot in my mouth. Not wanting to insult anyone, I finished all the food on my plate. To my horror, the division president saw how much I enjoyed the Chinese delicacies, so he restocked my plate with more. I put on my best smile and thanked him. Trying to keep the nausea from bending my smile, I stifled a hiccup between each slurp of blood curd soup. Yum!

A few days after returning to New Hampshire, I went to see the gastroenterologist for a follow-up visit. While checking in with the receptionist, she asked, "Has anything changed since your last visit?" I responded, "I am a little bit older." She chuckled, as did two other young office workers sitting behind the counter.

My meeting with the doctor lasted long enough for me to tell him that nothing had changed for the better. In fact, the hiccups were worse. I walked out with a prescription for a higher dose of antacids.

The demands of my job took me back to Hong Kong a few weeks later. I didn't mind, because the city fascinated me. On the way back home, the fifteen-hour flight from Hong Kong to Chicago turned out to be the flight from hell. The night before departure I ended up with a severe case of food poisoning. Fifteen hours in coach with bad diarrhea, hiccups and a bad headache—well, you get the picture. As soon as I was back in New Hampshire I headed to the stomach doctor. I walked out with a prescription for an even stronger dose of the same medicine. The hiccups had only gotten worse. By now it was mid-November.

My wife and I, with our son and daughter, drove to Upstate New York to visit her family for Thanksgiving. It's a 500-mile drive that we tackled once or twice a year for the holidays. During the meal, I was wrestling again with hiccups while trying to squeeze bites of turkey down my throat. Every piece that I did manage to swallow felt like it was too big to go down. Even the mashed potatoes put up a fight. Between the hiccups and difficulty swallowing, I couldn't fill my stomach.

In early January, I flew off to Vienna, Austria to my company's division headquarters. I was there to make an hour's presentation to my peers and corporate officers highlighting my year-end accomplishments, and my strategic plans for the year ahead. It would be difficult to suppress the hiccups while speaking. This was my fear: Standing in front of the entire management team, you feel like you are re-interviewing for your job. At this level in a Fortune 500 company, plenty of people want your job and would be delighted to see you fail. The sharks were always circling. My fear of failure was enough to scare the hiccups out of me.

The other managers present were friends, but all fierce competitors. We wanted our colleagues to be successful, but subconsciously no one liked it when someone looked *too* good. A bright star diminishes the shine of those around it. I was aware of some of the tricks used by others to make someone stumble, so I always turned off my cell phone before I stood at the lectern. I had seen a presenter stumble badly when one of his 'friends' in the audience dialed his cell phone in the middle of an important presentation. The corporate officers were not impressed when the presenter tried to turn his phone off and fumbled it onto the floor in the middle of his speech. My hiccups behaved long enough for me to survive my presentation, Power Point slides and all.

Later that month, while at home, I felt an odd sensation in my jaw. It was a relatively warm day, and Barbara and I were outside enjoying the fresh air. We were walking down our driveway, the only place in the yard not hidden under a foot of snow. Under our massive oak tree barren of leaves, I turned to her and said, "It feels like I went to the dentist and had an injection of Novocain. It's the same feeling as when the Novocain is wearing off. A cold, numb, tingling sensation." It was limited to a small area on the right side of my chin about the size of a half dollar. The sensation never went away. Days later the feeling had spread to my entire jaw. Over the next week, it continued to spread over my entire head, from my shoulders to the top of my scalp.

This development prompted me to make another appointment with my primary care doctor. He saw me right away. "My head feels like it's in a bucket of ice water," I explained. To the touch, my temperature felt normal, but my head felt freezing cold to me. The doctor looked perplexed and responded that even after decades of practicing medicine, "There's always something new." I told him that I didn't think this was a stomach issue. He agreed to send me to a neurologist.

By this time, I knew something was seriously wrong in my body. There was something going on in my head. Barbara and I talked about what it might be. We dismissed the possibility of a tumor because we weren't prepared to deal with such a thought. We were deeply in love, had two wonderful children, and life was good. There was just no room in our life for a brain tumor.

It couldn't happen to us.

2

On a Monday in late January, I sat with the neurologist in his exam room for several minutes. He was a wonderful, intelligent, kind man who listened carefully when I spoke. He did not rush the interview. He answered my questions with details and concern. And to my relief, my symptoms led him to believe that I had some kind of migraine.

I was about to reach for my coat when he added, "But just to be sure that there aren't any rocks in your head, I'll order a CT scan. No, I'll make that an MRI." He added, "If you don't hear from me for several days after the MRI, don't be concerned."

The next Wednesday morning, I drove myself to Parkland Hospital for the MRI. The technician was working busily behind the glass panel. After lying on a gurney and handing me earplugs, the nurse placed a needle in my arm so she could inject a contrast agent, gadolinium, into my veins during the scanning procedure. While I lay supine, she wheeled me into the confined space of the tube. Some people have to be sedated before having an MRI, and I can understand why. One feels confined and helpless. I could only see the plastic interior of tube about three inches above my eyes. The nurse settled a panic button into my hand just in case. I had had MRIs over the years for various other maladies, so this was nothing new to me. In less than a half hour, I was wheeled out of the tube and sent on my way.

As I was exiting the MRI room, that was when the look on the technician's face struck me. Why was he holding the door for me, and why the look? It gave me an eerie feeling. I dismissed it and drove the five miles back to my house, but in my heart, I knew that my life was about to change.

I worked from an office in my home. Vienna was a little too far from New Hampshire for a regular commute, so thanks to the wonders of modern technology, my division headquarters was simply a phone call, fax, or e-mail away.

After that fateful MRI appointment, I settled into my office to catch up on e-mail. The phone rang. Expecting a call from Europe, I picked it up rather than let it go to voicemail. It was the neurologist. Before he could finish a sentence my mind began racing. The last thing he had said to me as I left his office was to not be concerned if I didn't hear from him for *several days*. Then why has he calling me so soon? There could only be one reason. It couldn't be good news. He must have seen something with the MRI. How bad was it? My thoughts reeled, even as time seemed to slow down.

I processed every word he spoke.

I analyzed every tone and inflection of his voice.

When he said there was a mass in my brain, all the other words before it just vanished.

I thought, *What is a mass? Be more specific. I'm no doctor.*

And then he said, "You have a brain tumor."

When I heard that word, the voices in my head drowned him out. I could hear his words in the background, but they were garbled. My mind raced. It all made sense to me now. I had already begun to believe that something was wrong inside my skull. Of course it was a tumor. Why had I rejected that possibility? His voice faded away as the word *tumor* sunk in. He kept talking, but I stopped listening and didn't hear much of what else he said. The word *tumor* rang in my ears.

The only other words I remember him saying are, "It can be treated," and, "Your primary doctor has already been informed."

Barbara was at the local elementary school where she worked as a computer technician. Of course she knew

If You Love Me, Take Me Now

I was scheduled to have an MRI that day, but I couldn't call her just yet. For the next hour or so I was in shock. I could only pace back and forth in my living room. I kept moving, both body and soul. From one end of the room to the other and back again. My mind was running in overdrive. My heart was pounding, my thoughts racing, and I couldn't stand still. I just kept pacing back and forth. What had just happened? Had I been given a death sentence? Is this really happening? I wasn't just asking myself the hypothetical question, "What if?" I've seen movies where characters get a terminal diagnosis, but this was no movie and I certainly wasn't dreaming. My thoughts kept racing, and my feet kept carrying me back and forth between my desk and the door.

I wasn't fully aware of how, but I knew that from this point forward, my life was going to change in ways I never could have imagined. I had so many questions that had to be answered. Am going to die? What will happen to my family? What will happen to me? What do I do next? These are isolating, lonely questions. I broke down and cried. I hadn't cried like that since I was a small child.

After what might have been an hour of pacing, I collected my emotions and called my primary care doctor. The receptionist must have known to expect me; she transferred my call without putting me on hold. He greeted me with concern in his voice, and made it immediately clear that he had anticipated many of my questions, and had ready answers. *Are you sure it's a tumor? How big is it? What do I do now?*

From what I can remember of that conversation, he gave me two options. My insurance policy would fund either of two hospitals. I asked him which one he recommended and he said he couldn't do that. I knew both hospitals were world-class facilities, known to be leading hospitals in research and care. I chose one hospital solely because it was a shorter drive. I had nothing else to go on. It was Lahey Clinic in Burlington, Massachusetts.

I had already decided I couldn't break the news to Barbara over the phone. I'd have to wait until she arrived home from work. I knew that she'd be crushed by the diagnosis: a possible death sentence. Her life was about to change almost as much as mine. My heart was beginning to break by the visions I had of what her reaction might be. She was my soul mate, my co-pilot. I felt guilty because I knew this would hurt her. Still in a state of shock, I was unable to do much work for the rest of the day, and decided just to work out as many of the logistics as possible.

I placed a phone call to Lahey and eventually landed at a desk in the office of Doctor Carl. Unlike the long wait to see the stomach doctor, he could see me in two days—Friday. His receptionist asked me to bring the MRI photos. (They hadn't gone digital at Parkland yet, and still used film.)

A few minutes later I was on my way back to Parkland to pick up the films.

My next call was to my younger brother, Andy. He happened to be in an airport about to board a plane for South America. Like me, he worked for an international corporation, and his job also required extensive travel. I told him, "Do you remember me telling you I couldn't get rid of these hiccups? I just found out what is causing them." My mouth felt dry. "I have a brain tumor. Andy, I may be circling the drain." By his silence I could tell he was stunned. I could hear the airport intercom in the background announcing last call to board his flight. Our conversation was cut short and he told me he'd call me the following day from Argentina.

When people hear the two words, *brain tumor*, they think death. Rightfully so. The odds of survival are not good.

With nothing else to do, I went home to wait for Barbara.

Barbara and I had met on November 10, 1978. She was in the US Air Force and stationed at Pease Air Force Base in Portsmouth, New Hampshire. Like me, she had finished college in the middle of a recession.

Barbara studied art and jewelry design in college and degreed in Fine Arts. Even in a strong economy, it's hard to make a living as an artist. Barbara was self-confident and had an adventurous spirit. One day, a few months after graduation, she walked into an air force recruiter's office and listened to his sales pitch. He must have sounded convincing because Barbara signed her name on the contract and committed her life to the US Air Force for the next four years. She walked home and told her Mom what she had done and her Mom burst into tears. It was a spur of the moment event that changed her life forever.

After graduation I was unable to find employment opportunities in my field of study. Companies were laying off people and certainly not hiring new graduates with no experience. With no other prospects that summer I resumed my old job as a lifeguard on an ocean beach. In late October, long after the beach had closed for the season, I ran into Rick, a college roommate who was back in New Hampshire for a few days. He had moved to a ski resort town in Colorado and asked me if I'd be willing to share his apartment with him. He needed a roommate to help pay the bills. It took me about a nanosecond to make a decision and accept his offer. A few days later I packed my 1964 Volkswagen Beetle with all my worldly possessions and drove to Colorado.

It didn't take long for me to land a couple of jobs at the ski resort. On most days I was a fry cook at the small restaurant at the top of the mountain, about twelve thousand feet up. Other days I was a ski patrol. I made barely enough money to pay the rent and buy beer. It was a fun time, but I wanted more, so to increase my odds of landing a good job I spent the next two years in grad school back in New Hampshire.

One day about a year after I finished grad school, I was at a local watering hole listening to the band with the same Rick I lived with in Colorado. Rick's girlfriend walked in and sat down at our table. Accompanying her was this gorgeous brunette. For me, it was the quintessential love-at-first-sight. Barbara was quick to smile, self-confident, and intelligent. At twenty-five and in an active duty job, she was slim, and had long brown hair that reached her lower back. And for some reason that I couldn't understand, she liked me.

The next day, I called her to ask her out. To my surprise and delight she said yes. From that point on we started dating. She worked as a flight simulator specialist, and her schedule was varied enough that we could see each other frequently.

We married in May of 1979, seven months after we met, and never looked back—but I always wondered why such a gorgeous lady had wanted to date the likes of me.

She left the military after four years and we both found ourselves unemployed. The company I worked for went out of business. By now the economy had improved and we quickly found new jobs. Barbara's military training in electronics had qualified her for a good job with a military sub-contractor. I found a job with a commercial electronics manufacturer. From our apartment, we each had a long commute and the two companies were a good distance apart. One day it dawned on us that, between the two of us, we were now making just enough money to buy a small house and say goodbye to apartment living.

Together, we poured over a map and pinpointed a town at a location that split the distance between each of our employers. Before long we found an affordable house, bought it and settled into the community. We were young, life was good and we were in love. Our daughter, Amanda soon arrived and less than three years later, our son Nathan was born. Amanda took her dad's features with blond hair and blue eyes, while Nathan resembled his mother with dark hair and brown eyes. We were a family.

Time passed and now both kids were in college. Amanda was studying the arts, like her mom had, and

Nathan was studying technology. The apples didn't fall far from the tree. Barbara and I were treating our empty nest like a second honeymoon. We had started out life together with nothing and now it was treating us pretty well.

By now we had moved into a bigger house. We had it built in the same town several years after we moved there. The yard was much larger, eight acres in fact, and it was a wonderful place to raise our children. Enough room to have vegetable and flower gardens, pets and plenty of wild life to observe. Lots of space for kids to run free and explore the outdoors. Now that they were away in college, we would occasionally find time to spend a week or so on an island in the Caribbean. We both liked to travel and did so whenever we could.

Now I had to do something I dreaded. Having to hurt her with the news of a brain tumor tore at me. I wanted to hide it and make it disappear. A secret so devastating—even one that I had only kept from her for a few hours—could only be from a bad dream. It was the news that no human being on the planet wants to hear.

I waited, but she didn't come home at the normal time.

Too distraught to focus on my job, so I just sat in front of the television, worrying, wondering. The sound and picture on the TV screen were muffled and out of focus while my fears accumulated and controlled my thoughts. My mind was still exploring everything that had just happened.

She had planned to meet some gals after work for a glass of wine at their favorite restaurant. She had a group of very close friends, mostly schoolteachers, who met once a week to blow off steam. She'd often call me from the restaurant, and she did tonight. I wasn't sure how to respond if she asked me about the MRI. To my relief, she didn't bring it up.

At around 7 p.m., the doorknob rattled in its usual way and she walked into the living room. I was still sitting on the couch watching TV. She smiled, said hi and walked past me into the kitchen. A glass of wine and time spent with good friends usually brought her home in a good mood, and today was no exception. Still too scared to tell her the news outright, I walked into the kitchen after her. I asked her how her day was. After a few short pleasantries she asked how the MRI went.

"I have a tumor in the back of my head."

From across the room she looked at me with a sheepish smile and waited for me to say I was kidding. It would be like me to kid around just to get a reaction. It took her a split second to read my expression and realize this was no joke

She ran to me, hugged me, and burst into tears with her head on my shoulder. We just stood there, locked in an embrace, and cried.

And like that, our lives changed forever.

The MRI films were in a large manila envelope on the kitchen table. There were several dark negatives about 12 by 14 inches with multiple pictures on each sheet. We scattered them on the table and searched for the tumor. Neither of us had any idea of what we were looking at. The image of my brain was obvious, but what would a tumor look like? There was small white spot, about a half inch across, on the outer surface of my brain in one of the films. It was the size and shape of a grape. Maybe that was it. It was on the surface and appeared easy to remove, like a mole or awkward toenail. What did we know?

3

In the past few months, new symptoms had been appearing more often and with more intensity. A diagnosis was an odd sort of relief—no more chasing phantom stomach problems. I phoned the stomach doctor's office to cancel my next appointment. The secretary asked why and I told her about the brain tumor. She offered me best wishes and a sincere, "Good luck."

In the past ten years of working, I had taken a total of two sick days. One because I was sick, the other was for a job interview. The diagnosis had just rearranged my priorities. My boss reminded me frequently how important my work was. The revenues I brought to the company kept many people on the payroll. Those people in turn had spouses and children depending on them. I took this responsibility seriously. But now I needed some time to gather my thoughts. Time away from the office. My needs became more important than there's. The following day, a workday, I went skiing.

I had been a skier longer than I can remember. A few years before I met Barbara, I had worked on the ski patrol at that resort in Colorado. While in grad school I had a job at a ski area in New Hampshire. To me, skiing was second nature, like walking. Cruising along at 50 mph with the wind whistling past my ears was cathartic. It was a complete physical and emotional release.

Barbara's boss, after hearing the news, told her to take whatever time she needed, so we both played hooky and drove to the slopes together. It was in conflict with my work ethic, but at that moment, I was incapable of focusing on my job.

Barb and I got up early, made sandwiches for lunch, loaded our gear into the car and put our skis on the roof rack. We headed north on the highway for the two hour ride to the mountains. Being a work day, the roads heading north were not busy with eager skiers. As we passed by the exit we'd take to visit our daughter at school, our conversation drifted toward memories of raising our two children, how proud we are of them and how to approach them with the details of this new development.

Off in the distance we could see the mountains slowly rising out of the horizon as we put miles behind us. The tall pine trees were dark against the white snow and the ski mountain appeared in the distance with long white vertical stripes. The sky was deep blue as it often is on a cold winter day.

We arrived and parked our car, put on our ski boots and carried our gear toward the base lodge. The sun was warm, but the air was frigid with only a light breeze. The snow made a crunching sound with each step as it does when the air temperature gets below a certain point. Ice crystals glistened in the sun resembling flakes of diamonds on a bed of cotton. The beauty of the surroundings distracted the anxiety we were both feeling.

At the mountain, we met up with Rachel and Paul, a couple we had known for years. On the first ride up the mountain, enclosed in the four-person gondola, I said to my friends, "I have to catch you up on what's happening in my life." I paused to be sure I had their attention. "I have brain tumor." Rachel laughed. This was the second time someone had reacted this way. When neither Barb nor I smiled, she realized the mistake.

We skied for the rest of the day. We'd kick around the what-nows and what-ifs each time we shared a four-person lift. The questions were plentiful, but we didn't have many answers. On this crystal clear day, the height of the ski lift gave us a spectacular view of the mountain range. It sadden me that it might be a long time before I get to enjoy its beauty again.

The next day Barbara and I would find out more at Lahey Clinic.

Friday morning, we met Doctor Carl. He was a slight, soft-spoken man of about five-eight, about an inch shorter than me, and appeared to be about my age. After introducing himself he asked, "Why are you here?"

Annoyed, I answered, "Because I have a brain tumor."

Hadn't anyone told him? Shouldn't his nurse or secretary have briefed him? Should I have chosen the other hospital? These questions slammed through my thoughts, unfiltered because all my energy was going toward hiding my fear. I was here to discover my fate and his question intensified my anxiety.

"Yes, I know that," he said. "What are your symptoms?"

With my concerns stanched, I told him about the hiccups. He commented that he had never had a patient who presented with hiccups.

"Are you having a hard time swallowing?"

I hadn't connected the dots on that one yet. " I thought I was always just trying to swallow something too big."

"That's what everyone says." He gave me a slight smile.

Doctor Carl hung the MRI films up on a light panel, and pondered quietly for a few seconds as he looked them over. The white spot that Barbara and I had identified as the tumor was not a tumor after all. In the lower back of my brain, on the brain stem and crowding the cerebellum, was a large white mass. It was the shape Barbara and I had previously dismissed as being too big to be a tumor, and assumed it was supposed to be there.

The mass was about the size and shape of a large chicken egg. After what seemed like a long pause, Doctor Carl looked at me and said, "It *has* to come out."

I heard what he had left unsaid. It has to come out, *or you will die.*

I had already accepted the fact that brain surgery was inevitable. Surgery was the cure, the fix. But now it was more than just removing a small grape on the surface of my brain, but a large egg inside my brain.

Barb asked the doctor what to expect after surgery. He replied, "You may have double vision." To me that sounded like an easy recovery.

I asked, "For how long?"

"About three months."

Now I was getting concerned. How was I going to work with double vision? I had never taken three weeks off, let alone three months. What would my boss say to that? Did I have to worry about keeping my job? It wasn't what I knew that scared me, but what I didn't know. What were the questions I hadn't yet thought of to ask? What were the answers to these questions? I needed details, data, and information to apply to critical decisions.

I started to realize that there could be a major financial impact to all of this. Two kids in college, a mortgage, taxes to pay—all of the things that once seemed like the natural price of our comfortable life now loomed over me. My heart sank.

Half-kidding, I asked, "Can you do the surgery tomorrow?"

Before he could answer, Barb blurted out, "Don't you want to wait until after the Super Bowl on Sunday?"

I added, "Fine, how about Monday?"

Amused, Doctor Carl said, "I'll go check and be right back." I wanted to get it over with as soon as possible and get my life back on track.

A few minutes later he returned to the examination room. "I can't do it until February 24. Nothing will happen to you by then." I didn't feel good about a four-week wait, but I deferred to his expertise. He had already declared that he thought it was a slow-growing tumor. If he was correct, it wouldn't change very much in a few weeks. And at least I'd get to watch the Super Bowl. New England was playing Philadelphia.

In truth, the symptoms had been accelerating, and I left my appointment dubious that nothing would happen to me in four weeks. I hadn't voiced my concern out of respect for Doctor Carl's knowledge. That turned out to be a mistake.

The weekend before the diagnosis, Barb and I were invited to a small gathering hosted by one of her work buddies, Kathy. She and her husband, Bob, had a lake house about an hour's drive from our home. Being January, the landscape was covered with snow and ice and the lake was frozen solid. We brought our skates hoping it was clear of snow. The dirt roads along the shoreline were covered with packed snow and tricky under our tires, but we were eager to get away for the weekend.

I had met Kathy before, but never Bob. When we arrived, I carried a case of beer up the walkway to the front door. The path was icy. In a split second, my feet went out from under me, straight forward, and I landed flat on my back and hit the back of my head, hard, on the frozen ground. The case of beer landed square on my chest. I went backward so fast I wasn't sure what had just happened. I wouldn't know till the following week that there was brain tumor in my head that may have played a roll.

I lay there, stunned for a few seconds, while taking inventory of my bones and joints. Then I tried to get back on my feet. My body had cushioned the fall for the case of beer and saved it from leaving a layer of frozen foam on the walkway.

My head spun when I stood up and stars floated through my view of the remaining pathway. Dizzy and with a lump growing on the back of my head, Barbara led me to the front door.

The following Sunday, February 1, the weekend after the diagnosis, Bob and Kathy came to our house to watch the big game. When Kathy and Barbara were in another room, Bob said to me, "I hear you've had a bad week." He was among the first people, other than one brother, Rachel, Paul, and medical staff, whom I spoke to about having a brain tumor. It was a preview, a practice run, for what I dreaded. Eating me alive was the thought of having to tell my family, colleagues, and especially my children. The news was going to cause them pain. The news was going to hurt them all. I felt terribly guilty for what I had to do.

Even so, the afternoon of the Super Bowl managed to provide some levity. Bob and I were sitting on the couch watching Janet Jackson's performance during the halftime show. Bob's jaw and mine dropped simultaneously. We looked at each other and in unison asked, "Did you see what I saw?" Wardrobe malfunction—yeah right!

After the game Bob and Kathy drove a short distance to their home. I began to understand that the events unfolding were going to impact more people than just my family. I had to start informing the people who needed to know. Bob's casual reaction loosened me up just enough to spell it out in my head. After watching the big game with Bob, I was passing by my office door when I decided now was the time to draft an email. Otherwise I might be up all night worrying and thinking about it.

The upper management team was located in various places around the globe, so I'd copy an e-mail to all of them.

Subject: *Personal and Confidential*

To all,

I have to inform you about some news that will affect my ability to perform my duties as an employee. On Wednesday of last week I was diagnosed with a brain tumor. Needless to say, the last few days have been very emotional for me and my family. There is a mass on my brain stem about the size of a chicken egg. I have been experiencing symptoms for several months.

On February 24, I will have surgery to remove the tumor. I plan to continue to work until that time. While I was in Vienna a few weeks ago, the symptoms were at full strength, so you can see that I am still able to work.

If You Love Me, Take Me Now

There is a measurable possibility that the tumor and/or surgery will result in my demise. In that event, I ask that you provide emotional and financial support to my family. If all goes well, I should be back to work in three months or less after surgery.

Please tell only those who need to know. This is all new territory for me. Feel free to call.

Best Regards,

Steve Cox

I reread and sent the e-mail message on Monday morning. Barbara was at work, and in the stillness after the message was gone, I wondered how her day was going. Her task wouldn't be as easy as mine. She couldn't just hit the send button to tell her friends and colleagues. She would be informing them about our situation face to face, and have to practice subduing the emotions that had been overwhelming us both. I had never envisioned that telling friends and colleagues would be so difficult. I didn't want pity, I didn't want anyone to be saddened by our predicament.

A few hours after hitting the send button, my phone rang. It was Jim, my boss's boss. A Scottish national about my age. Even though we both spoke English, his heavy accent always made it difficult for me to understand him. The Austrians were *much* easier to understand, even though English was their second (or third) language.

Uncharacteristically, Jim was compassionate in his condolences. He asked what my plans were and I reiterated that I planned to work as long as I could. The conversation shifted to business issues and how to handle the dissemination of news. Specifically, the news about me. As a strategic account executive, I managed the relationship between my employer and an extremely important customer, a worldwide manufacturer of cell phones and Internet equipment. My company designed and built products that provided power to run the equipment the customer made, and I was the point man for a multi-million-dollar account. Jim and I agreed that it was important to provide a seamless transfer of responsibilities before I took my leave of absence.

My first priority was my family's well-being, and ironically, it made me keep pushing them down further on my list of people to tell. They always came first, but now, the very thought of telling our children brought tears to my eyes. The implications of my surgery were clear. The odds of surviving a brain tumor were not good, and

Barbara and I had to break the news to them that their dad had a brain tumor and might die. Amanda and Nathan were college students and mature enough to understand everything that meant. This was a task I dreaded.

Barbara and I agreed that a phone call was not enough. We'd visit both of them individually and help them through this. Amanda was in school about seventy miles from home—a round-trip drive we could easily make in a day. Barb called Amanda and asked if she had time to see us the next day for a short visit. We often dropped in to see her and take her to lunch or drop off something from home that she needed, so Barb's call didn't rouse suspicion.

The following morning we drove the seventy miles to the university. We took the same northbound route we had driven to the ski area, but we exited a few miles south of it. The day was cold, and blustery with wisps of snow-laden breezes that blew across the highway and occasionally obscured our view. We met Amanda in her apartment. She was renting a room in a small building on the edge of campus. The residents shared a common area with a living room and a kitchen. She introduced us to a few friends who were preparing their lunch in the kitchen as a few others were busy studying books laid flat in front of them on the kitchen table, and then we migrated into her tiny room down the hall from the common area. The room, packed with books, clothing and Spartan furniture was barely large enough for three people. I found a spot on the bed, while Barbara and Amanda occupied the two chairs.

We made small talk for a while before I said, "Mom and I have something important to tell you." She looked at us, silently waiting. "I have a brain tumor."

The expression on her face didn't change. It was as if she was looking through me and not at me. The color dropped out of her face. Nothing else was said for an uncomfortable moment.

"I'm going to have it removed on February 24," I added.

Her only reply was "Oh."

There was no emotional outburst, only an uncomfortable silence. I wasn't sure how she'd respond. She'd never been one to lose control of her emotions. She'd always been able to weigh her thoughts before responding and today was no different. On the other hand, she'd never been confronted with a family tragedy and had probably never anticipated news like this. Even so, her response seemed almost too composed. Maybe she did that for us. An outpouring of emotions would have pained us both.

I was relieved that it was done. I told her where the surgery would be and not to worry. We had a good doctor and we expected a good outcome.

After the visit with our daughter, Barb and I spent a quiet hour driving home. On this cold January day, the snow banks were high on both sides of the interstate. It was a gloomy overcast sky. Appropriate for our moods, as neither of us said much. I know we were both thinking of Amanda. We were both very proud of our children. They had developed into wonderful young adults that any parent would be proud of.

Barbara broke the silence with, "I wonder if she knows how dangerous a brain tumor is. She didn't say much." I thought for a second before I replied, "Maybe that's a good thing."

Our next visit would be with our son. He was in college about fifty miles from home in a different direction. We agreed that we'd give him a call when we got home and try to see him the next day. But for now, we were emotionally drained. We shared a pot of coffee in the kitchen, head in hand, slumped over the kitchen table. The phone was hanging on the wall beside us. Before I could reach for it to call our son, it rang.

It was Nathan, so I put him on speakerphone.

"Hi Dad, what's going on?" he asked.

"What do you mean?"

"Amanda's Facebook page says, 'Please pray for my dad.'"

My heart sank. Barbara put her face in her hands. We were going to have to tell him now.

"We were going to visit you tomorrow and tell you in person. We saw Amanda earlier today."

"I know, so why did she post that on her Facebook page?" he asked in a demanding tone. I sensed he was annoyed that his older sister knew something he didn't know, as if we were hiding something from him. His tone also suggested that he had no idea of what he was about to be told.

There was no way to avoid it. "Your mother and I have something to tell you. I have a brain tumor." There was dead silence. An awkward silence that seemed to last forever.

"What are you going to do?" His voice cracked with emotion.

We told him what we knew at that point, which wasn't much: the date of surgery and the hospital.

After he hung up I felt guilty and disappointed, as if I had let him down. My emotions didn't make much sense to me, but normality had left my life. I had never planned for such an event, nor even thought about it happening to me—happening to us.

I was only beginning to understand the impact this was having to the people around me. I wasn't the only victim here. As a family, all four of us were victims. Whatever my fate proved to be, it would forever impact the lives of all of us. Up to this point, our family life had been good. Other than a broken arm or a blackened eye, we had all been healthy. But now, life was taking on a different dimension. One with an uncertain future, an unpredictable outcome—foreign to what we were used to. As a family, it affected us all. No one would escape.

My physical health was in turmoil, and the emotional health of my family was at stake. They had the pressures of college to deal with. More than ever, for their sake, I had to be the strongest, most confident version of myself. Otherwise my anxiety would transfer to them and cause them more pain than they were already feeling. The timing could not have been worse for all of us.

My next phone calls were to my sister and elder brother. No sense in mincing words with them, either. Like everyone else, the news took them by surprise. My sister had the most emotional response of the two, and I thought I heard her crying. She regained her composure enough to ask, "What are you going to do?" I told her when and where surgery was scheduled and not much else. At this point, I didn't know much else. I parted the conversation with, "I've told everyone but Mom and Dad. I'm going to call them next."

Last, I phoned my parents. For reasons I still don't fully understand, it was the most difficult phone call to make, and I had already put it off too long. As a parent myself, the mere thought of outliving my children was a nightmare. I was about to call my parents and tell them that one of their children might die.

Mom and Dad were in Florida. As a retired couple, they lived like many people their age. They spent their summers up North and escaped the cold weather by wintering in the South. I had visited them only a handful of weeks ago. They were aware of my chronic hiccups and the difficulty I had eating. My father had witnessed me struggle with a sandwich in the club house in between rounds of golf. He watched me curiously and asked what the problem was. I told him I didn't know, only that it happens almost every time I eat. I made light of it even though they were becoming a major nuisance. Nothing else was mentioned and we went on to finish our round of golf.

Dad answered the phone. My heart was pounding. I didn't want to have this conversation. I asked him to put Mom on the other extension. Already, they knew that I had something important to say, and I felt the tension on the line.

"I know what is causing the hiccups," I began. "I have a brain tumor."

A few seconds passed in silence.

"Oh, you'll be all right." The response was shockingly casual. Maybe they were just trying to assuage my fear, or their own. Maybe they didn't hear me right, or maybe they just didn't get it.

I explained that I was scheduled for brain surgery on February 24. They said they would come home for the surgery.

After the call, I ruminated on the conversation. I realized they wouldn't have decided so quickly to make the trip North for something casual—it seemed they were already so much stronger than me.

Looking back, their relaxed manner should not have surprised me. They had raised four strong willed and competitive children. As time passed, there wasn't much that would fluster them. Once, as a teenager, I announced to them that I planned to hitchhike from our home near Boston to Colorado and back to do some mountain climbing. Expecting a stern, *no you aren't*, they casually offered, "Have a good time." Back then, neither I nor they fully understood the dangers of what I was about to do, and the journey I was now beginning was no different.

4

The next week was almost normal. I worked in my home office, and tried to concentrate on making a living. I slowly and selectively notified people that I would be dropping out of sight for a while. That's exactly how I told them: *I'll be dropping out of sight for a while.* On the list were old friends, colleagues, and a few customers. The last person on the list was a customer with whom I had built an especially strong relationship of trust and mutual respect. We worked together through both good and contentious times and learned from each other's professionalism. A friendship had grown out of it, and I called him directly but told him the same line: "I'll be dropping out of sight for a while."

Total silence followed.

"I have a brain tumor."

He groaned. For some reason his response hit me in the gut, and my reaction took me by surprise. The feeling he expressed with his groan broke the fragile barrier that held back my emotions. I fell apart and had to hang up.

Late in the week I had another appointment at Lahey Clinic, a pre-surgery appointment. It was mostly a time for me to provide proof of insurance, sign a pile of papers that indemnify the hospital and staff, and get all the legal mumbo-jumbo taken care of.

I also had to be examined by a nurse. I followed her instructions to lie back on the gurney while she checked my blood pressure and listened to my lungs and heart. Fine. Routine. But when my head relaxed on the pillow my head started spinning so violently that I thought I was about to vomit. I sat up in a hurry and the vertigo subsided.

This was a new one. Another symptom.

I asked myself if I was I going to survive the few weeks till surgery.

The nurse never smiled once. I was certain that I could read her mind, and that she believed she was examining a soon-to-be corpse. I was tempted to ask her if she could measure me for a casket, to lighten things up a bit, but thought better of it. Not everyone has my sense of humor.

The nausea returned when I got back to the car. We started to leave the hospital parking lot, but it got worse and I asked Barbara to pull over and stop. I opened the door and leaned out because I thought I might vomit. I didn't want to make a mess on the upholstery. We remained parked in the lot for a few minutes until the vertigo stopped. We thought about going back into the hospital, but what good would that do? At that point, I knew I wouldn't be able to work much longer.

From the parking lot I used my cell phone to call the head of human resources in my company. She was located in a different division but based in the United States. I was pretty sure my boss hadn't yet informed her about my situation.

She answered the phone and I repeated the words that had become my safe cliché, "Hi Holly, I'm going to be dropping out of sight for a while." She waited for the rest of the story without saying a word. I finished, "Jim (my boss) already knows."

"OK, Jim already knows? I'll take care of everything at this end."

Her unemotional response was both helpful and professional. It comforted me and her tone suggested that she knew exactly what to do. Clearing a path for a distressed employee is one of the tasked that she is trained to do.

Not much else was said.

Holly turned out to be a great help. Not until much later did I understand exactly how much she had helped me navigate the corporate and insurance labyrinth.

On the way home, Barb and I decided that we'd better get our wills updated.

We had written our wills many years before with an inexpensive software package. The wills were legal, but our lives, our family and our assets had changed over the years. I didn't want to leave anything to chance. If there were any loose ends, now was the time to get a good attorney to find and eliminate them. If I was going to die, I wanted to make my family's lives as uncomplicated as possible.

The two of us were now moving through life one part mechanically, and one part in a dream state, and both of us were thinking, "Is this really happening?" Yes, it was. We had to prepare for my death. The death of her husband of twenty-five years, the father of her children, her soul mate.

We approached each other tenderly, with compassion and concern. When we embraced, she hesitated to release me. When she held my hand, she did so tenderly. Our love was the foundation we had built our lives on, and it was now supporting a very heavy load.

A few days later we were in the attorney's office. She asked a lot of background questions. How many kids? Ages? Assets? And then the big one: "Is there any reason why you are having your will made at this time?"

"Yes, I have a brain tumor."

My answer didn't startle her or even evoked a flinch. I sensed that she had done this before. She had worked with couples whose lives were in upheaval. It made me feel confident that we had chosen the right attorney.

She didn't need an explanation. She didn't even ask any follow-up questions. They weren't necessary. "We'll get started and I'll see you back here in about a week."

I told her that surgery was scheduled for February 24, and the will had to be finalized before then.

Nathan, still in college, wrote an essay about his family for class. He sent me a copy. In it he wrote, "How could this have happened to me?" In this case, the *me* was Nathan. At first, my reaction was confusion, and, "It didn't happen to you, it happened to me." Yet once again, I couldn't escape the fact that my health had an effect on my family and close friends. It dawned on me how essential I'd become in so many small ways to so many people. Until now, this was simply my job, my role, a responsibility I took pride in: and now, for the first time, it looked like a liability. Even a curse.

It was happening to all of us, not just me. We all had this brain tumor. Everyone was in pain, searching for answers, offering support, trying to soften the pain and offer comfort. This monster had multiple victims.

Each day from then on was a bigger challenge. I could feel my body getting sicker. Sleep came is short sessions for both Barbara and me. Some nights we spooned in bed and just talked for hours, drifting in and out of sleep. Waking up to find the other awake.

I lost one or two pounds every day. I weighed 185 pounds in the beginning. Physically, I was in great shape. Before the diagnosis, besides the daily jogging, I played in a men's tennis league year-round. Occasionally I ran a 5K or 10K race. At fifty years old, I was in better shape than I was in my thirties, but now my body was beginning to shut down. My muscles ached, my mouth was dry, and even a short walk would force me to sit and rest. I felt ancient.

In the morning I'd wake up with a bad headache, vertigo, and nausea. Sometimes I'd have to sleep sitting up to keep the nausea at bay. My voice was getting hoarse and raspy, and speech was harder. Swallowing food was becoming more difficult, too, and compounded my weight loss. Every morning I'd step on the bathroom scale and be missing a few more pounds.

About fifteen days before surgery, I notified my boss that I was no longer able to do my job. My sickness was accelerating on a downward trajectory. At the rate I was declining, I began to worry that I may not make it to February 24. I had barely enough energy to walk from room to room.

A few more days passed and it became impossible for me to swallow any solid food at all. Barbara would prepare soup for me, and I'd have to pour it down my throat. It wasn't easy but it was the only way I could get nourishment in my body. I must have aspirated some soup into my lungs while I was trying to get it in my stomach; I developed a bad cough as my lungs filled up with fluid. Barbara brought me to the emergency room where they gave me antibiotics. A few days later I was able to breathe normally again, at least during waking hours.

Sleep became agonizing. As soon as I dozed off, I'd stop breathing. A short time later I'd wake up gasping for air, catch my breath, fall sleep, and then start the cycle all over again. My autonomic brain functions were beginning to fail. While lying beside me, feeling helpless, Barbara would sometimes just watch me and cry.

The hiccups kept getting worse. One day, while Barbara was at work, I called my primary doctor to ask in a raspy voice if there was something that could be done for the hiccups. His office answering machine took the call, so I left a message. "This is (hiccup) Steve (hiccup) Cox. I'm ha(hiccup)ving more and (hiccup) more hic(hiccup) cups. Is there (hiccup) any (hiccup) medicine (hiccup) that will make them (hiccup) stop?

His office must have contacted Barbara because she came home with a prescription inhaler device for me. She told me, "The doctor prescribed this for the hiccups. Hold it up to your mouth, push down and breathe in a blast of the vapor." I did so right away. I couldn't take them much longer. I was relieved just to see that there was a medicine for them.

I did as instructed and breathed in a lungful from the dispenser.

The medicine didn't work. It actually had the opposite effect.

Almost immediately, the hiccups starting to come faster and faster until there was one every three seconds. I couldn't speak, and it became hard to breathe. Each hiccup pounded a sharp pain into my diaphragm. The only way I could breathe was to time the hiccups. I'd take in a breath with the contraction of my diaphragm by using it to pull air into my lungs. I started to panic when I wasn't getting enough air. My fear made me pull harder after each hiccup until I could fill my lungs. It was painful, but it was the only way I could keep myself from choking to death in my living room.

Seeing my distress, Barbara got on the phone to the doctor's office. I didn't hear the conversation, because I was too busy concentrating on getting enough air. She said something to me and darted out the door. Twenty minutes later she was back home with a new prescription, something that would counteract the inhaler medication. It was in pill form and I managed to get one down my throat.

For the next eighteen hours, I still had to fight for breath: up all night and into the next morning, no sleep, just hiccups, exhaustion, and mild panic. By mid-morning, my breathing was back to "normal." Eighteen hours of a hiccup every three seconds. Eighteen hours of fighting for air. I was exhausted and finally fell asleep—only to wake up gasping for air.

Our children were away at college and had no idea of the trauma unfolding at home. No one knew the struggle we were facing except our doctors. It wasn't that we were masking the events, we were just too distracted to include others.

By now, I was convinced I was going to die. Each day was worse. I could see where this was going. Surgery was less than two weeks away, but the end felt closer than that. Barbara called Lahey in desperation. They were unable to change the schedule. People, rooms, and special equipment were needed and were already committed to other patients. We discussed the possibility of changing hospitals; looking back, we should have made that attempt. Our thoughts, probably incorrect, were that the whole process would have to be started over again and we'd lose our place in line at Lahey. We didn't know if I'd continue to fail as rapidly as I already had. After all, the surgeon had told us, "Nothing will happen to you…"

In retrospect, my symptoms made sense. The tumor occupied much of the fourth ventricle in the lower back of my brain and was adhered to my brainstem. This is where the human life support systems are situated. Motor and sensory neurons travel through the brainstem to relay signals between the brain and the spinal cord. It allows you to control your body, and also regulates functions that you don't have to think about, breathing, digestion, alertness, blood pressure, and heart rate.

In the brainstem are the nerves responsible for taste sensation, swallowing, and tongue movement. Their home base is square at the floor of the fourth ventricle: under the tumor.

In the next few days, my consciousness was fuzzy. Something new was happening. I can only remember very little about what transpired. I remember seeing and hearing Barbara making phone calls to doctors, pharmacists, and more doctors. I was awake, then I wasn't, and then I was again. During lucid times, my head pounded and I my body felt stiff. It felt like there was a metal rod running up though my spine and right through to the top of my head. I lost track of time.

I vaguely remember waking up, as if from a very long sleep. Barbara was standing over me with a worried look, studying my face.

She was saying, "You're back."

While I was out, the doctors had decided that my brain was swelling. Barbara gave me doses of a steroid, little by little, until it started to counteract the pressure in my skull. As the brain swelling subsided, I began to function again. If she hadn't acted fast enough I'd be dead today, because I was beyond the ability to care for myself. She saved my life—which now depended more than ever on getting in for my surgery.

It was midwinter. The roads were often icy and snowstorms were common. The Lahey Clinic was forty miles to the south. On any given day, commuter traffic could be a snarl. Missing my surgery date because of a traffic jam or a snowstorm was unthinkable. The husband of Barb's colleague was a Marriott executive, and arranged a complimentary room for us at the hotel nearest the hospital. It was so close it was within walking distance. No snowstorm or traffic jam would cause me to miss my date with Doctor Carl.

The final night before surgery, Barb and I ate a peaceful and pensive meal together at the hotel. The hospital staff instructed me not to consume anything within twelve hours of the surgery. Little did I know that my meal of blueberry pancakes smothered in maple syrup would be the last for a long time. A very long time. My ability to swallow had recovered somewhat, as long as I stuck to soft food. The pancakes were soft enough to wiggle down my throat. For the first time in my life, I could imagine being a death row prisoner enjoying a final repast. We ate in silence. Barb's fear was palpable, but I was relieved to still be alive before my execution day, and be close enough that a snowstorm or traffic jam wouldn't cause my demise.

Sleep that night was fitful. I woke once to the sound of Barb crying. We held each other in bed and contemplated where our lives were headed. Would she still have a husband by the end of tomorrow, or would she be making funeral arrangements? Would our children be fatherless? If I survived the surgery, what would I be like? Would there be any long-term damage? Personality changes? Physical disabilities? I wished this was all a bad dream, but it wasn't. These were real possibilities. I regretted that I had failed to ask Dr. Carl these questions. Once, the cancer diagnosis had seemed like a bad dream. We stood on the threshold of a major dishevelment in our life, and now, looking backwards a few months, the real dream seemed like our happiness. Our worries had been so trivial. Our material possessions no longer had value. The house, the cars—all were worthless, meaningless.

Our love for each other mattered more than anything. I told Barb I loved her and thanked her for being a wonderful partner. Tears rolled down her cheeks onto the pillow.

5

February 24 arrived cold. Barb and I didn't say much to each other while we showered and dressed. I could tell she was in pain. Every time she looked at me, tears welled in her eyes. I felt guilty; I was the cause of her discomfort. No matter that none of it was on purpose—it was me who made her cry.

We checked out of the hotel and found our car in the parking lot. Being less than a half of a mile from the hospital, we needed only a few minutes before we walked into Lahey Clinic and toward the bank of elevators. One whisked us to the surgical floor. My mother and father greeted us in the waiting room; my son and daughter were there already, too. No one smiled. Anxiety showed on their faces, reflected from mine and Barbara's.

We sat quietly, stealing peeks at the other people in the room. I wondered about their circumstances. What disease had brought them here? Certainly, they all had a unique story to tell. It couldn't be a good one. Fear was evident on their faces, as plain as it was on mine.

Doctor Carl appeared from a hallway around the corner. He was looking for me. I hadn't spoken to him since our first meeting four weeks ago, and he simply was coming out to be sure I had arrived as planned. He smiled, greeted me and introduced himself to my parents and children.

A few minutes later, a nurse appeared and called my name. I froze for a second and thought to myself, "I've made it this far." This was the surgery to save my life, but I felt like I was being called to the gallows.

Barbara gave me one last hug. Our children were filled with fear and sat like frozen statues. Fear coursed through me as I approached the nurse. She directed me down a narrow hallway. There was a small changing area where I stripped naked and donned a hospital gown. A few minutes later Barb appeared around the corner with the nurse, and the three of us walked through the doors into the operating room.

Barb stood next to me as I positioned myself on my back on the gurney. A male doctor, the anesthesiologist, began to set up some equipment next to me while another nurse was finding a vein to plunge a needle into. The doctor asked me if I had had breakfast.

I said, "No."

He said, "I'll give you some right now." I was surprised; but then he said, "Here it is," and injected something into the tube that was attached to the needle in my hand. It was the first time Barbara and I had laughed for a while. His demeanor helped us immeasurably.

A nurse told Barbara it was time for her to go back to the waiting room. We kissed and she left. Without warning, I was anesthetized and everything just went blank.

What seemed like a fraction of a second later, I awoke in the recovery room. I had been in surgery for nine hours, but the time hadn't registered. It was just lost.

I wasn't prepared for what I awoke to. Never having walked this path before, or known anyone who had, I had nothing in particular to anticipate. The surgeon hadn't told me what to expect other than possible double vision. Every surgery is different when it comes to brain tumors, so I suppose it's not practical for doctors to try to predict the outcome. I had a vague notion that I'd wake up after surgery and feel groggy. I'd spend a few days in the hospital recovering. A few days later I'd be wheeled to the exit door, walk across the parking lot and be driven home by Barbara.

As I emerged back into consciousness, I found myself in the recovery room, and the first thing I felt was pain. Excruciating pain. It engulfed me so completely that

I wasn't sure where it was or where it came from. My body ached all over. My head pounded. I lay on my back, gradually regaining my senses. My mind felt foggy, as if I was underwater. It seemed like a second ago I was talking to the anesthesiologist. A nurse was standing over me calling my name. A mask was over my mouth and nose, sending a mist of warm, moist air to my face. The nurse told me to take deep breaths, so I did as instructed. From both of my hands, needles protruded and led via a tube to bags of clear fluid hanging beside the bed. Further down, I could feel a catheter in my penis. Plastic tubes brushed both of my nostrils. A nurse told me to breathe out as she pulled them from my sinuses.

I had severe double vision. The one nurse was two. The two nurses were four and all of them were spinning around the recovery room, nauseating me. I felt as if I was dreaming, but the pain told me it was no dream. My right leg, however, was numb. I dismissed it—before the diagnosis, I had suffered similar symptoms stemming from back problems.

Continuing my inventory, my tongue felt like a balloon. When I tried to move my tongue side to side or up and down, it wouldn't respond. I could coax a little movement, but not enough to form words.

After a while, as I continued to take inventory of my being, I discovered that I couldn't swallow. Saliva accumulated in my mouth and drooled down my face. My entire right side, from head to toes, had a numb and tingling sensation. I can best describe it as the numbness one feels when you fall asleep on your arm and cut off the blood supply.

Barbara appeared at my bedside. She looked tired and pale. She asked me how I felt, and all I could do was grunt a few unintelligible syllables.

After being anesthetized, I had been rolled over onto my stomach on the gurney. While I laid on the operating table, Doctor Carl had cut a four-inch line from the middle–back of my head down the back of my neck. He then separated the muscles to expose the base of the skull. He cut a window in my skull to access my brain. To find the tumor, he had to push the cerebellum aside. The cerebellum plays a role in giving you a sense of balance: something that I would later find I no longer had much of. With his instruments Doctor Carl sucked out the tumor from the inside out.

He later told me he went after each and every tumor cell "aggressively," including those attached to my brain stem. If he had chosen to avoid the brainstem, tumor cells would be left behind to multiply and grow. Had that been the case, my recovery would be easier, but I'd have to deal with a tumor again and possibly have more surgery and radiation. Instead, he chose to go after it all. As a result, during the resection the tumor, my brain stem had been traumatized. The nerves so important to human life had been compromised. It was a tradeoff, but knowing what I know now, I'm thankful he chose that path.

At some point I was moved out of the recovery room to a floor that had several rooms running down each side of the hall. A nurse's station was at the end of the hall. The IVs were still attached to each of my hands.

Once settled in my new digs I fell in and out of sleep, but never a restful one. I'd doze for an hour or so and then return to fuzzy consciousness. It was a small room and I was the only occupant. A television hung from an arm attached to a wall. A big clock faced my bed. My window looked out at a brick wall a few feet away but also allowed a glimpse of the snowy parking lot a few stories below. I could see people going about their business. Presumably their lives were normal, unlike mine.

During the second night in that room, sometime around 2 a.m., long after Barbara had gone home, I asked a nurse if I could get out of bed and walk. My speech was barely legible. She helped me get up and then steadied me. I clutched the metal pole on wheels that accompanied me everywhere; hanging from it was an assortment of IV bags.

I managed to take a dozen or so steps down the hall, turn around and make it back to my room. All the time with the nurse and the pole at my side. It was an exhausting trek, but at least I was mobile again. My head hurt and my body ached. Being on my feet accentuated the numbness that now encompassed my right side from head to toe. My muscles tingled painfully with each step, and with double vision it was hard to focus my eyes. I struggled with balance, but managed to get back in bed.

The next night, in between snippets of sleep, I asked the nurse if I could take another walk. Again, with her help, I made it to my feet, still attached to a tower of bags. Out into the hall we went. A few steps later, I vaguely recall hearing a lot of commotion and a female voice yelling for help. The next thing I remember is sitting on a box on the floor surrounded by nurses and a male doctor.

It didn't register right away what had happened.

When I was back in my bed I asked the nurse what all the commotion was for. She told me I had passed out and fallen backwards. She caught me on the way down—tower of medicine and all. She was a petite woman and it took all her strength to prevent me from falling onto the floor. It reminded me of the day at the lake house, when the back of my head slammed hard on the ice. Except that today, the back of my head was a railroad track of metal stitches. She was the one I heard screaming for help. By the time I came to, they had me safely sitting on a box on the floor with my head between my legs.

That was the last time I attempted to walk for the next few weeks. Something in my blood pressure control system had gone awry. Why it took two days to stop working, I can't explain. Trauma to the brain stem is an elusive culprit.

To this day, I wonder whether the brain tumor or the surgery caused me more problems. I was much sicker after surgery than before, but the brain tumor would have killed me in a few months. In short, the tumor required surgery; the surgery caused brain damage; but the alternative was death. Simply put, the tumor was the primary source of the damage and therefore the cause of all the problems.

A few days later the surgeon informed me during his rounds that the pathologist had determined that the mass he removed from the fourth ventricle in my brain was an ependymoma.

"A what?" I mumbled.

An adult with an ependymoma is a very rare patient. The incidence of ependymomas is higher in children than in adults, and ependymomas are a small percentage of all primary brain tumors (Figure 1). A primary brain tumor is one that originates in the brain, as opposed to one that metastasizes from elsewhere in the body.

Figure 1

Distribution of All Primary Brain and CNS Tumors by Histology (N=158,088)
CBTRUS Statistical Report: NPCR and SEER Data from 2004-2006

- Craniopharyngioma .7%
- Embryonal, including Medulloblastoma 1%
- Ependymomas 1.9%
- Oligodendrogiolas 2.1%
- Lymphoma 2.4%
- Astrocytomas 6.8%
- Nerve Sheath 8.7%
- All Other 12.7%
- Pituitary 12.7%
- Glioblastoma 17.1%
- Miningioma 33.8%

Gliomas (ICD-O-3: 9380-9384, 9391-9460, 9480) account for 32% of all tumors and 80% of malignant tumors

Brain tumors are classified according to the presumed cell of origin. The two most common types of cells in the nervous system are neurons and glial cells. Glial cells are the supportive cells of the brain, and tumors arising from these cells are called gliomas. An ependymoma is a rare type of glioma. They are thought to develop from cells that line the ventricles (fluid-filled spaces in the brain) and the central canal of the spinal cord. Dr. Carl told me he was certain that he removed all of the ependymoma.

6

For the next several days I felt progressively worse. The headaches, the body aches, and the fog in my head all thickened. The numbness and the burning and tingling sensation at the top of my head went all the way to the bottom of my right foot. The entire right half of my body, head to toes, was almost unbearable. The nursing staff would not give me any painkiller stronger than codeine. They told me that after a brain trauma, anything more powerful could be harmful.

My mental state was deteriorating as well. The hours passed by at an agonizingly slow rate. No distractions could keep my mind off the pain. I felt like I was in a struggle to survive, and if I merely decided to die, I could. My depression never fell so deep, though—it just scared me that I was so close to the bottom that I could sink to a terminal depth if I chose to do so.

Because I was unable to swallow they provided me with a suction device to suck up the saliva in my mouth. It was like the one you'd use in a dentist's chair: a hooked tube that I'd hang from my mouth. It was the only way to prevent saliva from dripping down my chin and neck.

Trying to sleep with the hooked tube hanging from my lips was horrendous. It would fall out while I slept and I'd wake up in a pool of saliva on my pillow. I wondered how I'd ever share a pillow with my wife again. Would I be an embarrassment to my children?

Attached to my body with adhesive were several wires that ran to an array of electronic monitoring instruments beside my bed. One of my hands bore a needle and tube inserted in a vein, and my other arm had a needle and tube inserted in an artery. A bag of clear saline dripped down one tube and into my IV. A clothespin-type clamp gripped my fingernail to monitor the oxygen saturation of my blood. It was so tight that it would turn a fingernail black if I left it on the same nail too long. I moved it from fingernail to fingernail until all my fingernails became inflamed, then I'd move it from toenail to toenail. If any of the monitoring wires or tubes became loose, an alarm would sound at the nurses' station down the hall.

All I could do was lie there for hours on end, watching the hands on the clock creep around the dial. Sleep would last for an hour at best and then I'd be awake for an hour or two and then sleep again. This was the pattern every day for weeks. My back hurt from lying in the same position for hours on end. When I tried to get some relief by flipping over onto my stomach, I'd become tangled in the web of wires and tubes. Inevitably a sensor would pull off my skin and a nurse would come running in response to the alarm it triggered at the nurses' station down the hall.

There was a television in the room, but my brain was so scrambled that I couldn't watch it. Between the double vision and my inability to concentrate, the television would actually exhaust me. Trying to read a book had the same effect. I just couldn't do it. All I could do was lie there, thinking about my family, my job and how my life had changed while enduring pain, vertigo, nausea, and difficulty speaking.

Time slogged. Pain encompassed my entire focus. One morning while running my fingers through my hair I found small chunks of dried blood. To remove them I carefully slid them, one by one, to the end of the hair fibers that they clung to. That way I didn't send a tangle of hair along with them to the trash can. There was one chunk that tenaciously clung to my skull. No matter how hard I dug a fingernail into it, it wouldn't budge. When a nurse came in to check on me I asked her to see what was in my hair.

She parted the strands with gloved fingers and said, "It's a staple."

There was a metal staple stuck to my skull.

She said, "I'll get something to pull it out with." She came back a few minutes later with something similar to a pair of piers and yanked the metal staple from my head. My head had been held securely in a metal halo during surgery. The nurse speculated that the staple had been there either to help hold the halo in place, or to close a wound in my scalp made by the halo.

Days later I was still unable to swallow. I was losing weight rapidly, and watching my leg muscles atrophy. The surgeon visited me on his daily rounds and asked me to try. Nothing, nada, zero, zip. Not even the slightest muscles in my throat would cooperate.

More than a week went by as I lay in agony—tubes and wires shackling me. If I tried to sit up, my blood pressure would drop immediately. I'd pass out unless I kept my head at the same level as my heart.

Hunger and pain were my only thoughts. After the first full week of nothing entering my body other than saline and medications, a doctor told me they were going to insert a tube into me, through my stomach wall, to which they could administer some liquid nutrition. Wondering out loud to a nurse how much I weighed, she told me the high tech hospital bed I was lying in could weigh me.

She pushed the button to weigh me and told me the results. I was shocked, horrified.

Months ago, I had been an avid runner and had virtually no body fat. I had jogged five miles almost every day for a dozen years before I became sick. I had weighed 185, and now, I thought there must be something wrong with the scale.

I weighed 138 pounds.

Depression hit me hard. What had happened to my life? How long would I be in pain? Would I even live through this and go home someday? Would I be disabled? How are my children dealing with this? Is my career over? How will I provide for my family? Tears came easy and often. If the chronic physical pain did anything positive, though, it commandeered my concentration away from the emotions that were troubling me.

Barbara, God bless her, came by every day to see me. She had to drive forty miles each way, often in heavy traffic and bad weather, to get to the hospital. Our love for each other gave me the strength to survive. Even though she always maintained an upbeat and positive appearance,

I could see the strain in her face, the fear in her eyes, and feel her love for me in her being.

One day she brought an eye patch to help me cope with the double vision. It was black and held in place by a string around my head. It made me look like a pirate, but by wearing it, I got rid of the double vision, and some of the nausea along with it. I wore it for a few weeks until my vision gradually restored itself. As long as I kept my head level, my eyesight was good. If I turned my head sideways, or was lying down on my side, the double vision came back.

The fact that my vision had corrected itself somewhat gave me a glimmer of hope. My eyes were working. Maybe my speech would recover and I'd be able to speak coherently again. Maybe I'd be able to swallow. I wanted my life back, my career. I wanted to be a husband and a father.

In between these thoughts I'd break down and cry.

A nurse disconnected me from the bank of medical instruments and wheeled me down the hall into an elevator. The sudden liberty was a treat. A simple little pleasure, but it boosted my spirit to see something other than the clock on the wall and the window that looked out on a brick wall. A room with no view.

We were on the way to have a feeding tube put in place. I was hungry beyond belief, and the tube would end the hunger pangs. More precisely, it's called a PEG tube. Percutaneous endoscopic gastrostomy (PEG) is a method of placing a tube into the stomach percutaneously, aided by endoscopy. I didn't care what it was called. I just wanted something to eat. I'd happily settle for food in my stomach, even if it didn't get there the normal way. Finally, after a week with no nutrition, I'd be fed.

Into the elevator and out onto a different floor. Down the hall and into another room I was wheeled. This room had a window that gave me an actual view of the world outside. I could see the snow banks that were piled to the sides of the parking lot. The few people I saw outside were going through their daily routines, and they made me wonder if my days would ever be routine again.

My mind wandered as a nurse busily prepared me for the procedure. How good life used to be. Something as simple as to be able to walk through that parking lot and breathe the cold, fresh air now seemed akin to a day spent skiing. Not long ago, it would have beyond me to imagine the life of a hospital patient. Now I yearned for the simplest things in life: to walk across a parking lot, shovel snow off the steps of my house, eat a sandwich. It didn't matter how much money I had in the bank, or what type of car I drove. I'd give them all up if it would make me healthy again.

A doctor entered my new digs and introduced himself. He was all business and never relaxed into a smile. I listened as he described the procedure about to take place. I would be administered a mild anesthesia, just enough to put me under, but I'd still be close to consciousness. He would then snake an endoscope down my throat. An endoscope is a medical device consisting of a long, thin tube which has a light and a video camera at the business end. Images from the inside of the patient's body—mine—would show up on a video screen next to the gurney.

Using the camera, he would locate a good spot to push the needle through my stomach wall, from the outside of my body. He assured me that though this was a low-tech procedure, it was tried and true and always produced the intended results. The targeting was simple; after he guided the endoscope through my mouth down my throat, the light at the end of it would be visible through my abdominal wall. He'd mark the spot and push a needle and cord through to my stomach. He then would push a snare through a channel in the endoscope and use it to grab the needle from inside my stomach. The needle, cord, and endoscope would then be pulled back up through my throat and out of my mouth.

Outside of my body the PEG tube would be tied to the cord. With one end of the cord now coming out of my mouth and the other through a hole in my belly, about two inches north of my belly button, the doctor would then tie the PEG tube to the cord. He'd then pull the string coming from the hole above my belly button. The cord and attached PEG tube would snake down my throat, into my stomach and up to daylight though my abdominal wall. A bulb at the end of the tube would prevent it from being pulled all the way through. Once in place, I could finally get some food in my stomach, through the tube.

I didn't care if I'd be limited to liquid cuisine. I didn't care if I couldn't taste it. I was ravenous. The nurse began to send the anesthetic through the IV in my vein and I quickly went under.

In no time I was conscious again. As I came to, the doctor stood over me and explained that he was unable to finish the job. He had snaked the camera down my throat into my stomach only to find my stomach full of ulcers. He seemed a little perplexed until he read the list of medications I had been taking. One of them on the list, a steroid, was supposed to have been chased with an antacid. Without the antacid, the medicine caused ulcers on my stomach wall. The good news was that the problem was understood, and could be corrected with a regimen of antacids. The bad news was that it would take another three days for my stomach to heal.

Three more days of no food. Three more days of suffering. Three more days of dreaming of apple pie and ice cream.

Off we went, wheeling toward the bank of elevators, and back to my room without a view. My mental state was falling back into depression. Everything hurt. My career was in jeopardy. My wife and kids were pained just by looking at me. Every day was worse than the one before. Where was the light at the end of this tunnel? How could my life have come to this? I lay in bed and cried.

Barbara came by later that day. I could see in her eyes the toll this was taking on her. She looked tired. Her husband was struggling to stay alive. Back at home she now had to be both mother and father to our kids. They relied on her strength, and I, too, relied on the strength of her love.

On one occasion, Amanda accompanied Barbara on her daily visit. She found a day to leave campus and come home. When they entered my room, I sensed that Amanda was disturbed by the view of her father. The way she looked at me, I could tell she was uncomfortable seeing me in this state. With the weight I had lost, the muscles in my arms and legs had disappeared. My thick calves were mere sticks. The cheek bones in my face protruded. The view took her by surprise. It pained her to see me like this and she didn't want to be there.

At home, Barbara was trying to maintain an atmosphere of normalcy. Without a single complaint, she would push a snow blower to clear the driveway of snow, make sure the bills were paid on time, and do all the chores she was used to doing as well as mine. She emailed updates to my colleagues who were curious to know my status and when I might return to work. She stepped in and delivered on her vow of 'In sickness and in health'. She was an anchor of strength for me and our children.

Three days passed and I was once again wheeled to the room with a view of the parking lot. The same doctor joined in for another try with the feeding tube. This time it worked. After being put under, I remember being conscious just enough to see and feel him pull the tube up from my stomach through my abdominal wall.

The PEG tube was a foot-long flexible tube, beige in color, and with a stopper at the end. Finally, I would get something to "eat."

The hunger had exhausted me, and my body was withering. I wanted to feel a full stomach, but the nurse had control of the menu. Because my system hadn't dealt with digestion for such a long time, she would only give me very small portions. Next to the bed, on the medicine pole, hung a bag of light brown liquid. My breakfast, lunch, and dinner. It traveled down a tube connected to the PEG tube. At least I knew I wouldn't die of starvation.

I wondered what life would be like without being able to swallow, not being able to eat a normal meal. Meals are more than nourishment. They are a social event, and a business necessity. I envisioned myself occupying a space at a table, with no food in front of me while everyone else ate. Would I make them uncomfortable? How would I deal with the drooling? I couldn't imagine people tolerating a suction tube in my mouth at a business luncheon. I began to understand that life was not going to be "normal" again. What would the new normal be like? Would I be able to work again, in any capacity?

I was getting ahead of myself. Before I could even ponder that, I asked myself if I would ever be able to walk, talk, or swallow again.

7

All I could do for days on end was lie in bed. Mostly on my back, and sometimes on my stomach. The tubes and wires still made it difficult for me to roll into a prone position. If I raised my torso with the electric controls that tilted my bed up, or if I propped myself up on elbows, the blood would drain from my head and I'd pass out. Both of my legs were inside inflatable balloons that were continuously being inflated and deflated by an air pump hidden under the bed. Every few minutes, the buzzing sound of the air compressor would begin and the airbags would inflate. The intent was to keep the blood flowing to the upper part of my body, and to prevent it from settling in my legs where clots might form. Wires, tubes, balloons. A blood pressure monitor on a timer would periodically inflate a collar around my arm. The hours crawled. I'd drift off into sleep for short naps and look up to see the clock had not advanced much. This was my new normal.

My brain was still incapable of reading or even watching television. It could not concentrate on anything for very long. I could observe, but not think. The only exercise my brain got was the attempts to memorize the names of the nurses so I could greet them personally when they appeared for their shifts.

I developed a deep appreciation and admiration of nurses, both male and female. How could anyone not feel warmth toward someone whose sole intent was to keep you alive and to make you as comfortable as possible? Nonetheless, I had one roommate for a few days who would give the nurses grief at every opportunity. The very people who were looking out for his welfare! It takes a special person to be a nurse, and a person I don't understand who would not be grateful for their help.

Weekends were particular lonely. The staff would thin out, understandably, to spend time with their families and live their own lives. The thought of not having that time with my own family fueled my depression. Barbara would appear every day, though, and occasionally I'd have a visitor or two.

Trying to stay alert and communicative for visitors exhausted me. Sometimes I was unable to stave off sleep and I'd doze off only to wake up to an empty room. As much as I enjoyed friends and family, they were sometimes too much for my body.

On most days, a member of the hospital staff would vacuum and pick up around my room. The cleaning staff was mostly Haitian—men and women who had come to America in pursuit of the American dream. I'd greet them by their name, if I recalled it. I looked forward to their daily friendliness.

At that time a political uprising in Haiti was beginning to unfold. The news on TV would show snippets of the crisis as it was heating up. The 2004 Haitian coup d'état grew out of conflicts of several weeks during February 2004. It resulted in the removal from office of President Jean-Bertrand Aristide. One of the Haitians on the cleaning staff would stop working and watch the TV in my room whenever news of their homeland came on. He and I had become friends, and he knew I didn't mind.

After a few days of this, more and more of the Haitian staff would gather in my room, close the door and watch the news of their homeland. I enjoyed the company. They trusted me not to expose their unauthorized work break.

My blood pressure, or lack thereof, still prevented me from walking, let alone sitting up. My brain stem was still healing, and so were the biological controls that managed my blood pressure. If I simply hung a leg off the edge of the bed, my blood pressure would drop. My head would spin and my vision would cloud over as if I was looking through a very thick fog. Sometimes a white ring would invade my vision. I could see beyond the outer edges and through a hole in the middle, but the ring itself completely blocked my view. I dubbed it the "white donut."[1]

Most doctors I've visited seem to have never heard of this before. But one doctor, an orthopedic surgeon, listened as I described my blood pressure problems. Before I had a chance to mention the white donut, he asked me if I ever see the "white bagel." He understood!

Those taking care of me wanted to study my blood pressure problem. One day, a few people I hadn't seen before wheeled a contraption into my room. It was similar to a gurney: a bed-sized platform with straps and a thin mattress on it. At about the same height as my bed, it pivoted from the center point. There was a frame under it with a joint midway along its length so the head and foot of the platform could be raised and lowered from the center point. There were a couple of young female nurses and one guy who appeared to be in his late twenties. I don't know if he was a nurse or a resident. He was good-natured and explained through a foreign accent what they were going to do with the tilt table.

---

[1] As I write this many years later, the white donut still visits me when I stand up too fast. I've learned to quickly sit down. If I don't sit, I'm going to hit the floor, hard. I almost fell down a flight of stairs once when I fought the donut. I passed out and hit the floor at the top step.

He and the nurses lifted me on to the "rack" and strapped me in. They reattached the wires to my chest along with a blood pressure cuff on my arm. They were going to measure my blood pressure while they tilted my body up and down.

First, they took note of the readings on the instruments before they started their experiment. I lay flat, strapped to the tilt table, as they slowly pivoted my head up and my feet down. In silence, they all watched my blood pressure readings on the monitor. As they raised my head, my blood pressure would drop. When they bought me back to the supine position, my blood pressure climbed. I could feel it happening. When my head was higher than my feet, I grew faint. Several times they pivoted my head up, a little higher each time. Each time, they brought me closer to unconsciousness.

During the highest point of what turned out to be the last pivot, I said, "I'm going to pass out."

They reacted by quickly bringing me back to horizontal. The blood must have rushed back into my brain, because it felt like my head was going to explode. I screamed with pain as they watched me writhe under the straps. I had never had such an agonizing headache as those few minutes. I begged the nurse for a shot of codeine, but she refused. According to her it would have been too soon since my last injection.

A few long minutes later, the headache subsided. I felt exhausted.

After that incident, I was lifted back into my bed and I fell asleep. At some point I woke up again to the room with no view and that clock on the wall. I felt miserable. Life couldn't get much worse than it was right now.

Back in the time when I was a healthy father, husband, executive, and human being, there'd be the occasional bad day in my life. To lift my spirits, I'd remind myself that someone else, somewhere out there, was having a much worse day than mine. I had no idea who that someone was, but the reminder would help me put things in perspective and put me in a better mood.

Here in the hospital, my method of self-therapy didn't work. I couldn't imagine someone else having a worse day, a worse week, a worse scenario. Sometimes I'd just lie there and cry.

The days all melted together. I lost track of what day it was. A doctor told me they'd be moving me to another hospital soon. A rehab hospital. It was in Southern New Hampshire and much closer to home. At least Barbara wouldn't have to drive so far. As soon as a bed became available, I'd be moved. I guess the staff at Lahey had decided that they had done for me all they could. They had removed the tumor and kept me alive postop. Now it was time for occupational and physical therapy. The rehab facility would provide the therapy and time would take its course.

It was late March now and still cold outside. The day I was moved, they bundled me up in layers of blankets, and strapped me to the gurney. Lying flat on my back, the only skin exposed to the world was my nose, cheeks, and eyes. Once again, I was wheeled to the elevator.

Lying flat, I could only see the ceiling as the wheels clunked toward the exit. An ambulance was waiting to transport me.

It was the first time I had been outside of the building in weeks—not since that short morning drive from the hotel. I waited for a few minutes, strapped to the gurney under the sky on the loading dock, while they readied the ambulance. The fresh air was very cold and at first difficult to breathe. It was dusk and snow was falling. The flakes landed on my face and began to melt. Just being outside, feeling the cold air, the snow on my face, made my eyes well up with tears.

After I was loaded into the back of the ambulance, it began the forty-mile trip north. I was not going home, but I'd be closer to where my friends and family lived. That alone was a comfort.

Being late in the day, it was rush hour. We were traveling the route I had taken hundreds of times as a commuter. Traffic was heavy, but cars made way for the ambulance they saw approaching in their rearview mirrors. The siren was silent, and I don't know if the emergency lights were flashing, but we made good time. Any other vehicle would have been mired down in the highway congestion. As a commuter, I had seen the occasional ambulance navigating the congested artery during peak travel times. Sometimes I had wondered what their mission was—whose life was in trouble or who they were transporting.

Never once did I ever envision myself being inside it.

Upon arrival at my new room, the usual web of wires and tubes followed me closely as I rode down the hall to my new home. The suction tube was connected to a vacuum pump, which rode along with me. A group of both male and female nurses carefully lifted me off the gurney and onto my bed.

Barbara appeared a few minutes later. She caught me up on news of how life was proceeding at home, at her job and with the kids. Small talk, mostly, but comforting. Her friends were helping her with meals and household chores. The kids were doing well in school. We talked as the nurses checked the wire connections and secured the IVs in my hands and arms. I still had a suction tube in my mouth and a PEG tube dangling from a point a few inches above my belly button.

My tongue still felt like it was balloon in my mouth, and the words I tried to make were hard for most people to understand. Barb could decipher most of what I said since she had had a lot of practice learning this new dialect of mine. When our friends asked about me, she would tell them, "He has all his marbles, but they are in his mouth." I appreciated her humor. She shared the same sense of humor I had. I'm not sure if I learned it from her or she from me. Or maybe it's one of the things that we both had that attracted one to the another.

8

The next morning I awoke to a room with a view. What I had always taken for granted in my life now made a difference. Outside I could see trees in their winter bareness. The small yard between my window and the forest was covered with snow. The sun shone off of it and blinded me until my eyes adjusted. My mood adjusted, too.

Other than that one small pleasure, this place was just another hospital. A TV hung on the wall, but my brain was still too foggy to watch it. Five minutes and I'd be exhausted. Tubes and wires still tangled with my limbs when I tried to lie on my stomach and the catheter pulled on me uncomfortably. At least I had a view, and at least Barbara's life would be a little easier. Small consolation, but a step in the right direction.

The daily routine was the same, albeit in a new venue. Shots in my belly, a prick to a finger to check my blood glucose, codeine every few hours, pills, IV fluids, and light brown breakfast/lunch/dinner pushed through a tube in my belly. This was my life.

The pain, the vertigo, the tubes and wires, the lack of mobility, the fact that simply sitting up would make me pass out, the inability to swallow—it all dragged on my mental state. Before this, when I was healthy, I had heard of depression, but never understood it. I questioned if people who suffered from depression were just weak-willed. Why couldn't they pull themselves out of it? Now I understood. Life does get that bad. I was so low that not a day went by without my crying in solitude. Was this how it was going to be? Was life as I had known it over? Had I gone from provider to burden?

Days passed, and then one afternoon I managed to swallow. Once only, but it was a sign of healing. I'd have to concentrate to make it happen, but then I could do two in a row. The right side of my throat started to work. Over a few days, I regained the ability to swallow my saliva. No more drooling. I retired the suction tube.

A control console on my bed let me raise and lower my upper body. My blood pressure began to stabilize enough for me to be able to raise my head up without passing out. However, when I tried to sit up with my legs dangling over the edge, I'd have to lie back quickly or I'd faint. Even while lying on my back, if I simply hung both legs over the edge, I'd start to faint.

Over a few days I found that if I carefully eased myself into a sitting position, however, I could do it. First, while lying flat on my back, I'd hang one leg from the knee down over the edge. Even this simple action would make my head reel. After my body recovered, I'd position myself to hang two legs over the edge while still lying flat. The first few times I tried two legs, I had to pull them back up onto the mattress to stay conscious. But after several tries over a few days, I could stabilize with two legs over the edge. With that accomplished, I'd sit up on the edge of the bed for a few seconds until I knew I'd pass out if I didn't lie back down. Eventually, I could sit up. The whole process would take me ten minutes or more. First the one leg, stabilize, the second leg, stabilize, and then sit up slowly. A week or so of this and my body finally allowed me to sit up at will.

I was still shocked at the amount of weight I had lost. My thick calves were gone and my cheekbones were protruding. The "hearty" meals being pushed through the tube into my belly were just enough to sustain me. Even though I could partially swallow when I concentrated on it, the nurses would not allow me to take a drink of water. The threat of aspirating some fluid into my lungs was still a concern. I felt thirsty all the time and did sneak an occasional swallow until one nurse caught me. She wasn't very happy about it, and administered a scolding.

Now that I could sit upright, I could maneuver my way into a wheelchair. This gave me mobility and a new freedom. I still had to make my moves very deliberately; while Barbara and a friend were visiting one day, I tried showing off my new ability to get into a chair, and promptly passed out. They both helped me back into bed and kept the incident a secret from the nurses.

Even though I had mobility, it still didn't give me freedom to use a toilet. Because of my total lack of balance and the blood pressure problem, standing up was impossible. I hadn't mastered the task of muscling myself onto a toilet, so a portable urinal and bedpan were brought in.

The wheelchair allowed me to explore the hospital beyond my door. When Barbara showed up for her daily visit, I had her wheel me outdoors and around the parking lot. It was a sunny but cold winter day with a berm of snow circumventing the parking lot where the plows had pushed it. Even though I was covered with a heavy blanket, I froze until I shivered. Cold had never bothered me before like it did now and it reminded me that I was still very weak.

I was outdoors for the second time in weeks. What used to be routine in my life now felt like a gift. My view changed from the four walls of my room to a different landscape around each corner of the hospital. The cold made my body feel alive again, but it did accentuate the fact that my entire right side, from head to toe, was numb. I thought of people I had seen in shopping malls getting around in wheelchairs. This was their daily existence, and now I understood.

My outlook began to improve. I could swallow again if I tried hard. I could sit up, and I could move around. None of the things that I used to take for granted was easy, but the developments helped my depression subside. Hope rewarded with progress was the best medicine I had been given in weeks.

My daily routine began to change. My physical improvement qualified me to participate in physical and occupational therapy. After all, this was a rehab hospital. Its goal was to rehabilitate me to the point where I was healthy enough go home.

Once or twice a day, I was wheeled down the hall to a large room with tables, exercise equipment, and even a mock kitchen. I'd be given simple tasks to perform, like placing round pegs in round holes. My wheelchair and I would be placed in front of a machine with two handles that reminded me of pedals on a bicycle. I'd be tasked to turn the handles as fast as I could for a set amount of time. In this way, I started to rebuild my strength, stamina, and cardiovascular health.

These excursions gave me the first close look at my neighbors in the ward. Their ages ranged from early twenties to elderly. No one spoke of what malady had brought them here, and the nurses weren't allowed to answer questions about other patients. I assumed many had been stroke victims. The younger ones could have been in serious car accidents. I could only wait in my room and guess.

My speech was still slurred and difficult for people to understand. My right side was numb. I could not balance well enough to walk. I presented with many of the same symptoms as someone who had had a stroke. A tumor, a stroke—the brain damage often looked the same.

Each day, before I was wheeled to the therapy room, a nurse would remove the inflating and deflating balloons from my legs and pull therapeutic socks over my feet and legs all the way to my crotch. She'd then wrap them with an ace bandage. They squeezed my legs tightly to keep my blood in my upper torso and from pooling in my legs. One morning, one of the nurses who had been taking care of me put socks on me and began wrapping my legs in the bandages. I complained to her that she was wrapping them too tight and they were uncomfortable. She made light of it, ignored my complaint and wheeled me off to therapy.

As I sat there I could feel my feet getting cold from lack of blood flow. When she brought me back to my room, I told her once again that this pair of socks were too tight and were cutting off blood flow in my legs. She placed a hand on a foot, confirmed what I had said and started to unwrap the bandages. They came off too quickly, and the blood raced back into my legs. The blood drained out of my head and I passed out cold.

My blood pressure dropped so far, so fast that my body shut down. I don't know how long I was out, but when I woke up, there was a doctor hovering over me and a very embarrassed nurse. She was almost in tears. She was young and only trying to do her job, but I hoped she learned to listen to what her patients told her.

Speech therapy was also on my curriculum. I'd sit with a therapist who taught me various tongue movements to strengthen and help me regain control of my tongue. She had me practice moving my tongue side to side and up and down, and touching my lips with the tip my tongue – and saying, la,la,la,la and da,da,da. These were natural movements and sounds that I had never given a second thought. Now they took effort and concentration. The things that most people take for granted were difficult for me. Never did I imagine that my life would come to this.

Each day brought improvement to my ability to swallow, until I was eventually able to eat soft foods. The PEG tube had to stay with me for eight weeks, however, to complete a healing cycle before it could be removed.

At first, I could swallow once if I concentrated. A few minutes later I could do it again. Eating normally would take a while, but it was a possibility again. One day, I was wheeled into a lab room for a close inspection of the workings of my throat. I was placed in front of an X-ray machine with a monitor that we watched as I swallowed applesauce. The applesauce was laced with barium, an element that absorbs the X-rays and shows up on the monitor as a bright white blob. While I swallowed the applesauce, the doctor watched the motion and movement of barium. The right side of my throat appeared to work correctly, but the food was getting stuck in the left side.

Peristalsis on the left side just didn't work—and has not worked since. But eventually I would be able to eat again if I was careful.

9

Physical therapy began to focus on restoring my balance and strength. With assistance from a therapist and a lanyard tethered around my waist, I'd place each hand on two parallel bars about waist high, put my weight on both feet, and try to walk while supporting myself with the bars. It was exhausting, but I needed to be able to walk again. I gave it everything I had.

Before long, I could walk with one hand on a railing in the hall while an attendant held the lanyard wrapped around my waist. I graduated to walking down the hall without holding on to the railing, but still tethered and using a cane. Sometimes I'd lose balance and bounce a shoulder off the wall and the attendant would keep me from falling over. After many days of practice, I was allowed to walk untethered, but I still felt unsteady and fearful of falling. None the less, this was progress. A few weeks before I could not swallow, walk or even sit up in bed. Now I could walk – with a cane. I was mobile again.

My blood pressure was—and would remain—a problem. If I raised my head up too fast by sitting up or standing, I felt the blood draining out of my head and would have to sit down fast before I fainted. If I look upward, or turn my head quickly, I went into a spin. Poor balance made the cane indispensable.

A few days shy of five weeks after surgery, I was released back into the real world. Barbara came to pick me up. Gaunt, I walked out of the hospital, cane in hand. We walked across the parking lot and I climbed in the passenger seat. It would be a long time before I felt stable enough to get in the driver's seat. The time spent between that last drive to Lahey Clinic and this drive home had been a nightmare, a living hell. They had been the most difficult five weeks of my life. I felt fortunate to have survived, but I still hadn't understood how much my life had changed.

During the ride home it all started to feel like a dream again. A very bad one. I was re-entering in the real world and I desperately wanted my life back. I held back tears as Barb pulled into our driveway. For so long, I feared that I'd never be here again: never be able to eat a sandwich, never stroll in the gardens around our house, never smell the mist of a warm summer rain. Just to be able to roll over in bed without being tangled in tubes and wires was a magnificent new freedom. A simple freedom I had never before brought to mind.

At home, I began to see what Barbara's life had been like without me. Our friends had truly stepped up to help her. The refrigerator was filled with casseroles, pies, and other donations from people who just wanted to help. For the next few days, several friends stopped by the house with even more delightful offerings, lasagna, and chocolate cake. It had been a long time since I had tasted apple pie. I set out on a mission to regain some of the weight I had lost.

During my hospital stay, I had tried to stay in touch with my employer in Vienna. Barbara updated them on my progress while I was incapable of communication. Two days after I came home, I told my boss that I'd start work again, but only on a part-time basis. My belly still had a PEG tube dangling in front of me, my balance was very poor, and my speech was horribly slurred. I couldn't walk without a cane. Looking back, I wish someone had told me to take it slow and delay going back to my job; my brain was muddled and my ability to think clearly was still awry, but I wanted my old life back so desperately. Being an executive in a tech firm was my identity, my old life.

My job gave me a level of pride and self-worth. There was no pride in being an invalid or burden on my family.

Barbara noticed that I was still struggling with even the simplest tasks. She asked me how I felt.

"You'll never fully understand what I've been through unless you experience it yourself." I told her I'd been to Hell and back. I was back, but not all the way back. Exhaustion kept me from working at a pace I was once used to. Frequent naps caused unfinished paperwork to pile up. The medications I was taking aggravated the fatigue I always felt. Barbara thought I was trying too hard and told me so, but she didn't get in my way and try to slow me down. Sometimes I wish she had.

But she was right. "Part-time" was impossible. I was the liaison for my employer and a few of its most important customers. Millions of dollars of business flowed through my home office. Being so remote, in a home office, my employer could not see my physical condition. They could not see me stumble when I walked, nor the tube in my belly, nor how I was struggling with exhaustion and depression. They could, however hear my speech, or lack thereof.

As soon as people knew I was back at work, my phone rang from Europe before 7 a.m. and from China after 9 p.m. and from everywhere else in between. The e-mails poured in and my dream of working part-time accelerated to full speed. Not faster than it had been before, but faster than I could handle. Jumping right back in, I soon was traveling to Canada, Austria, and Ireland. Barbara, and even my doctor, warned me that I was pushing myself too hard. To me, there was nothing hard about taking a bus to the airport and sleeping in a coach seat at thirty thousand feet. I had always found those times in my past to be relaxing, so I wasn't dissuaded. Before long, I wish I had listened to them.

In between flights from Calgary to Ireland, I had a layover for a few hours at Heathrow Airport near London. In the executive lounge, I found some time to relax and do some computer work. With Wi-Fi access, I connected my laptop to the Internet. After checking e-mails, I ran a search for information about ependymomas. Whenever possible, I would read everything I could find about brain tumors. I wanted an answer to the question that had deviled me all those weeks in a hospital bed: Why me? Was it from cell phone use, something in the environment, heredity, or some pathogen? I needed to know.

I clicked on a link to a support group. I wanted information, and these people should be able to help. I also yearned for someone to talk to. Someone who had lived what I had lived. Barbara was always willing to listen, give her opinion, and feel my pain, but she hadn't walked in my shoes.

People I talked with, a casual acquaintance or a close friend, were typically uncomfortable talking about my situation. Talking about it helped me cope with my fear and sadness, but nobody wanted to hear about that. Without an outlet for my emotions, I often found myself in tears, in private, feeling very lonely. This online support group might be the answer.

They kept a secure e-mail list, so I had to e-mail the moderator and ask permission to join.

From Heathrow I flew to Cork, Ireland and taxied to a subdivision of my company. My corporate peers hadn't seen me in many weeks. Not since my last visit to division headquarters in Austria. In Ireland, we all assembled for an annual sales meeting. I insisted on being there, even though no one would have blamed me for not coming. They were all sympathetic of my story. I thought I was doing OK until a few close colleagues suggested that I take more time to recuperate. My speech was still imperfect and impossible to hide. The cane at my side further emphasized my struggle. I was beginning to feel that I had made a mistake.

A few days after I returned home, there was a message welcoming me to the online ependymoma group. The members instantly accepted me into a very exclusive club that no one ever wants to join.

These people understood. They had been there themselves. Over time I got to know many of them, but only through my laptop.

One member of the group was a young woman who also had a 4th ventricle ependymoma. Not all ependymomas invade the 4th ventricle like ours had. She maintains a web site documenting her experiences. Her precise and articulate description of her battle with the beast gave me both sadness and joy. Sadness because I understood her suffering, and joy that I had discovered someone else who knew intimately my experience. Her story was *my* story. I could have plugged in my name in place of hers. She knew what I knew. She suffered what I suffered. She assuaged my loneliness by proving that I was not alone—not the only one. She described my poor balance by writing how "It feels like my body keeps going one way when I turn to a different direction." She wrote about the feeling in my head which "is a foggy, cloudy feeling in my head that affects my perception of the world around me. It's different from the headaches that grab me in that it is not pain. I describe it as cobwebs or as a feeling that I'm underwater." She also knows the "numbness on my right side along with a pins and needles feeling that never goes away." Those are her words, but I own them as well.

It gave me an odd sense of relief to know that I was no longer alone with my grief. There were people willing to talk, and more important, listen. I was living proof that misery loves company. I became a regular contributor to the group and a recipient of their knowledge and comfort. I vented my emotions and garnered support—and so did they. They understand like most others can't.

10

Still under doctor's watch, I had an appointment with an ear, nose, and throat specialist to evaluate my difficulty swallowing. The left side of my throat never fully recovered. While sitting in the hospital exam room, I asked the doctor, "What are we going to do today?"

He looked at me, perplexed, as if to say, *No one told you?*

"I'm going to snake a camera down your nose and throat."

I was thinking, *Oh wonderful. It's probably a good thing that no one told me.*

The doctor held a device, similar to the endoscope used to place the PEG tube in my belly. At the business end was a small lamp and a camera lens. The lamp would illuminate the way and the camera would project an image on a monitor beside me. I sat upright during the procedure to keep my nose, neck, and throat aligned.

With the assistance of a nurse, he inserted the shaft in my nose as I held my head back. By holding on to the sides of the chair, I staved off the vertigo I would normally have.

I could feel it pass into my throat as it traveled. The nurse told me to hold my head still, but by sliding my eyes to the left, I could see the inside of my throat on the monitor.

Theoretically, a puff of air could be blasted from the business end of the shaft. The doctor would use this feature to see how sensitive a particular area in the alimentary canal might be. If the puff made the patient jump or wince, it would give the doctor some indication. Today, the puffer was not working. Instead, he instructed the nurse to use the end of the shaft to tap my vocal cords.

She did so as he watched for a reaction.

He asked her to tap again.

On the monitor, we could see the device bouncing off of my vocal cords. I felt nothing—nothing at all. There was no longer any feeling in my throat. One more area damaged by the tumor.

"If I had done that to anyone else, they would have vomited," said the doctor. He then asked me to make an *eeeeeeee* sound which opened up my vocal cords enough for him to push the shaft right through. We watched on the monitor as he ventured down, toward my stomach.

When he was done with his expedition down my neck, he gently pulled the shaft straight up, out of my nose. As he did so, he mumbled that the other doctors wouldn't believe what just took place. He noted that he saw some acid erosion, and wrote me a prescription for an acid blocker.

For me, it was just another day of being invaded by some medical device.

Barbara and I made our way down the elevator and to the parking lot. The PEG tube was inconspicuously tucked into my underwear, otherwise I got strange looks if it hung out from under my shirt and dangled in front of me. I began to feel something warm slithering through my underwear.

In the privacy of our car, I unzipped my pants to inspect what was going on down there. I found the source of the warm feeling. The stopper on the end of the PEG tube had come off and my stomach contents were draining into my underwear. Oh joy! I'd have to sit in this for the forty-mile ride home. Over the next few weeks, the stopper came off a few more times.

Though uncomfortable and somewhat disgusting, these little annoyances in life seemed so trivial after what I had endured. Contrarily, life's simple pleasures energized my spirit more than ever. To be able to eat an apple, walk in the sunshine, and wake up next to my wife were blessings I had never appreciated as much as I once believed I had. My life was slowly returning to normal, and it felt good.

Still intent on learning all I could about brain tumors, and specifically ependymomas, I read everything I could find: the rate of occurrence and re-occurrence, the probability of getting an ependymoma versus other tumors, and the survival statistics. These are numbers that can be easily assembled from any large pool of brain tumor patients, and hence were readily available. What was difficult to find was a generally agreed-upon standard for postsurgical treatment.

As someone who had recently had an ependymoma resected from my brain, I wanted to do everything I could to minimize the possibility of its return. What therapy or treatment was going to give me the best chance of survival? I knew in my soul that what I had already endured was the most difficult ordeal I had experienced in my life. If another tumor grew, I doubted I could survive it twice. I didn't have the strength, and considering my mental state, I questioned my fortitude.

The little information I could find suggested that postsurgical radiation was standard. Many patients I read about had followed this protocol. Many of them also had stories about the side effects of radiation, and none had a happy ending—loss of hair, loss of hearing, and even loss of teeth years after treatment.

I queried the online support group for their opinions and knowledge. Many had radiation treatments after surgery. Others had not. I was unable to build a consensus from them because there was no clear pattern. With some who had radiation their tumor grew back, and others had no regrowth after radiation. The same held true for those who chose to avoid radiation. This was a small, unscientific sample, but it was all that I had to go on.

My surgeon was confident that he had removed every last cell of the tumor from my brain and that radiation was unneeded. Even a single cell left behind might grow into another tumor, and I wondered how he could be so certain he had found them all. I sought out a second opinion to help me decide if radiation was in my future. I told the surgeon I would be doing so, and he graciously understood my concern. I had been a little worried that he might take it as a personal affront, but he didn't.

It wouldn't have mattered anyway. It was *my* life I was protecting.

After making some inquiries, I made an appointment with an oncologist at a nearby hospital. I didn't want to make the trip to a Boston hospital, as it was only for an opinion, not a medical procedure. The nurse brought me into the doctor's office, where he was already seated at a large wooden desk. He asked me why I was there and I told him I was looking for the best course of postsurgical treatment for a brain tumor.

He asked me what kind of tumor I had, and I answered, "An ependymoma."

He paused for a long time, as if searching his mental database for an answer.

"I went to Harvard Medical School and have been practicing medicine for twenty-five years and I've never even heard of an ependymoma." Then he added, "I can't answer your question. I'll do some research and let you know in two weeks."

It struck me that day how rare ependymomas are. My research had found that most occur in children. Adult ependymomas are extremely rare. Among all primary brain tumors that occur annually in adults in the United States, less than 2 percent are like mine. In raw numbers, that's about 1,800. As time passed, more than one doctor told me they had never heard of an ependymoma.

Two weeks later I sat again opposite the oncologist at his big wooden desk.

He said, "I spoke to Doctor Carl, your surgeon, and we agreed that you don't need radiation."

My first thought was that this was not exactly an independent second opinion, but I took his advice, thanked him, and left his office. Knowing the survival rates of those who had radiation versus those who did not, and the potential side effects, I weighed this information with his (albeit influenced) opinion, and decided to forgo radiation. On one hand, I wouldn't have to worry about the damage. On the other, I'd worry about a second tumor.

It was a risk I chose to accept.

11

Elsewhere in the family there was some bad news. Suzanna, my uncle's wife, had been diagnosed with a brain tumor. She was not a blood relative, so no one wondered if cancer ran in the family. She lived about twenty-five miles east of us in a quaint coastal community, and it was unlikely that the two of us could have be exposed to some dangerous agent in our environment. Nonetheless, it was tragic news. Hers was a glioblastoma multiforme: the deadliest of the deadly.

Back at the office, things were not good, either. I had been back at the job for several weeks when my gossip antenna started to pick up signals that something was amiss. My responsibilities were being slowly usurped and given to someone else. My effort to regain my old life through my career was stumbling. I had returned to the workforce much too early and my performance could not compare to what it was. I was still very weak and it was obvious to my employer from several times zones away. A colleague told me that he had heard that I was going to be replaced.

Such is life in a corporation. All the business I had developed was soon handed over to someone else, and I was demoted. The message was clear. My days as an executive were over. The damage from the tumor had taken on a new dimension.

It wasn't an easy decision, but I tendered my resignation. To my surprise, my employer asked me to stay on for another eight weeks, and told me to tell no one I had resigned. I think they were doing damage control. How would it reflect on them to push me out, a star performer, a family man who had suffered and struggled to pick up where he left off? Their altruistic façade might be dented if they kicked me to the curb too soon. I pulled the plug about three weeks shy of the eight weeks they wanted. They weren't very happy, but I didn't feel I owed them much at this point.

Barbara was still employed, but her salary was not enough to pay every bill. We had savings, but with one child still in college, we'd burn through the account pretty fast. Life had taken another turn for the worse. Depression hit me hard again and I'd find myself in tears for a spell almost every day.

The online support group helped me through some of the difficult times. When I felt down, I would pour out my feelings to them through my keyboard. There was solace in knowing that they could understand from a perspective that others could not. They offered empathy and advice, and in return I responded to their triumphs and grievances. I became an active member.

It was now September; eight months after surgery. The PEG tube had been removed, and it left a deep scar. One day while visiting my brother, he teased his youngest child, my eight-year-old niece, "Uncle Steve has two belly buttons."

She responded, "He does not."

I said, "Yes I do. Do you want to see it?"

She nodded, so I pulled up my shirt enough for her to see two belly buttons: one in its normal spot and the other about two inches higher. Her eyes widened and she turned and ran off toward a neighbor's house.

A few minutes later she reappeared with a band of friends all about her age. They all gathered around and looked at me, not saying a word.

I knew what they wanted, but I wasn't about to lift my shirt in front of a bunch elementary school kids. I envisioned myself being dragged off to jail and charged with indecent exposure.

"You'll just have to take my niece's word for it that I have two belly buttons."

They went home, disappointed.

My balance was still poor and I'd periodically have spells of double vision. I didn't feel very safe behind the wheel, so Barbara assumed full responsibility for driving. I'd occupy the passenger seat and annoy her with my complaining that she was going too fast or was too close to the car in front of us. I wasn't a good passenger. Much of my criticism was generated by the frustration I felt for not being in control. Not being healthy enough to take over the wheel and resume my former role.

She wasn't averse to telling me to, "Shut up!" And when she did so, I'd do exactly as I was told. After more than two decades together, I know when I had overstepped my boundaries.

It was now painfully clear that my life would never return to the old normal. I had held a job almost continuously since I was twelve years old. At my first job I made one dollar per hour pitching bales of hay on the back of a moving truck in the sweltering heat. That job ended when I fell off the truck and broke my arm.

Come to think of it, my executive career ended in a similar manner.

For the next year, I worked on regaining my speech, and aimed to reach a point where my impediment was not obvious. I wanted to be able to walk without bumping into things or falling over.

One day I was buying a light bulb to replace the one that had burned out in our car. I was tired, and my speech was still slurred and labored. I asked the store clerk for help locating the bulb. He got a big kick out of mimicking my speech, and even got a laugh from the other store clerks. It angered me, but people like that are doomed by their own cruelty and stupidity. I paid for the bulb and walked out to my wife who was waiting in the car. I didn't think it was even worth telling her about it.

Just walking in a straight line was a challenge. It still is. A fellow brain tumor survivor described it perfectly: When walking, it feels like a rope is attached to your head, and at the other end is a bowling ball swinging randomly. It pulls you one way and then another as you walk. It was sometimes difficult to avoid walking into someone who was approaching from the opposite direction on a narrow sidewalk. The bowling ball always seemed to swing in that person's direction just at the wrong moment.

My time was also taken up by tapping resources to help us regain financial stability. When my former employer hired me, the human resources manager asked me if I wanted the medical insurance package. I declined because I was covered under Barbara's insurance, and it was a better policy. Now, one of the financial resources I wanted to tap was a long-term disability insurance policy I had opted for when I was hired. Back then, the HR manager had asked me if I wanted it and at first, I said no; after a few seconds, I asked her if many employees buy this insurance. She said they didn't. After a few more seconds, I asked her how much it cost. The price was reasonable, so I said, "I'll take it" while I was thinking to myself, "You never know when you might get hit by a bus." As it turned out, I got hit by that bus.

Trying to collect on a disability policy deserves a book of its own. The hoops one has to jump through are intended to discourage you from pursuing a claim. It began with the insurance company denying that they had any record of my policy. Before long there were private investigators hiding in the bushes around my house taking videos of me. I understand that they have to protect themselves from fraud, but it would take an ingenious actor to falsify a brain tumor—or at least a very masochistic one.

Meanwhile, Barbara headed off to work every day. I'd visit physical and speech therapists a few times each week. Our daughter had graduated from college and moved to

Florida and found a good job. Our son was still in school. My life had turned upside down, and I could see no way out. Some days, while I was home alone, I would just sit in the house and cry.

12

Barbara ran the computers in the school system, and even though the students were on summer break, that time of year was very busy. It was the time to upgrade the software in every desktop computer and do hardware maintenance.

School reopened every September and one of her tasks was to train the teachers on the features of the new software she'd installed over the summer, as well as keep the computers in working order throughout the year. She was good at the job and enjoyed her responsibilities, but above all, she had a group of close-knit friends at the school—and they were what she really loved about it. Her pay was a pittance, but we could survive comfortably on what I had made when I was employed, and besides, her job gave our family a very good health insurance package.

Not long after school reopened for the new school year, Barbara developed a sinus infection, or so she thought. Her eyes were bothering her, too. She said they were itchy and painful. Though I showed my concern, I didn't pay much attention. There was nothing unusual about getting sick when all the kids came back to school. It was a roiling cauldron of childhood disease.

I suggested that she see an eye doctor, and made an appointment for her. The optometrist checked her eyes and deemed them healthy. We didn't think much of it.

My health was slowly improving, but I was still a permanent copilot in the car. I had attempted to drive, but found it difficult. My right foot was numb and I could not feel the pedals. I had a tendency to stamp on the gas, sending the car lurching dangerously into reverse. Roughly speaking, the same was true for the brake. I felt like a teenager learning how to drive. I practiced sensing the position of the pedals and easing my foot forward, but for safety's sake, Barbara did all of the driving except for short trips to the grocery store or the bank.

Barbara was especially sensitive to the times when I criticized her driving skills. To me, they seemed to be getting worse ever since she took over that responsibility, and this made me a much bigger pain in her ass. Her driving speed kept getting slower and slower, and I'd tell her she drove like an old lady. She would growl back at me, "I *AM* an old lady."

At fifty-two years old, she wasn't an old lady to me. Apart from driving annoyingly slowly, she'd sometimes drift leftward into the opposite lane, causing oncoming cars to swerve around us. Sometimes she'd barely miss hitting street signs on the left side of the road when turning in that direction. I'd lose my patience and yell, "You almost hit that!"

One day, her driving was so bad that, fearing for our safety, I demanded that she pull over and let me drive. She was so mad she wouldn't talk to me for the rest of the day.

October was upon us and my life—our lives—were slowly settling into the new normal. The old normal had vanished. Barbara and I were trying to enjoy the empty nest again. Our daughter had been successfully launched to a life on her own, and our son was finishing school. We had been married for twenty-six years, and in spite of the past year of hell, we were still passionately in love. Without her determination and dedication, I might have not survived to see the leaves change color on the trees and breathe the crisp autumn air. I had such a strong admiration for her. I apologized for yelling at her the previous day and told her I love her. She accepted my apology and said she understood how frustrating the changes in my life must be. Never could I have found a better partner.

School settled into its daily routine for Barbara. In between classes she chatted with friends. They were mostly teachers or worked in the school library. Her best friends were a group of seven others who shared similar interests. They all loved to laugh, and they watched out for one another. They all knew the story of my battle with a brain tumor and were unendingly supportive of Barbara and me. Whatever we needed, they provided. True friends.

They sometimes spent a girls' weekend away at the lake house. I would have loved to be a fly on the wall, but I'd only get to see the occasional photograph taken of them having a good time. As the story goes, one evening, fueled by their favorite libation, cosmopolitans, they all removed their bras and hung them on the railing on the loft above the main room. They declared themselves the Bra-Bra Sisterhood (after the Callie Khouri movie, *The Ya-Ya Sisterhood*). From that day on, the group of eight was known as the Bra-Bra Sisterhood.

Back in the halls of the elementary school, a few of them noticed that Barbara had begun to walk with a limp. She seemed to be dragging her left foot. Neither of us gave it much thought. Soon, though, Barbara began to complain that she was having difficulty controlling her right hand. Her dexterity with a paintbrush was not what it should have been.

A day or two later, we were getting ready to go out to a local restaurant for dinner. I was waiting for her to get ready and come down stairs so we could leave. I called to her and she did not respond. I found her in our bedroom standing with a blank expression on her face. When I said, "Hey! Let's go," she snapped out of whatever trance she was in and we went on our way.

Over dinner, I asked her what that was all about. She couldn't recall what I was talking about. It was all very strange, but I let it pass.

By mid-November her limp was not improving, nor was the dexterity of her right hand, nor were her sinuses. At this point, Barbara and I did a kitchen-table diagnosis of her symptoms. What could have gone awry in her body? The conversation was eerily similar to those we had about my hiccups and frozen head. As with that mystery, I felt uneasy not having an explanation. Sometimes *not* having an answer is more stressful than learning the cause.

We both considered the possibility that she might have had a mild stroke. What else could it be? What else would cause these symptoms? We didn't allow our imaginations to drift too far. If it was a stroke, that was bad enough. We didn't want any more bad things in our lives. We decided that she should see our primary care doctor.

A few days later she made an appointment. He was intimately knowledgeable about my health history, for he had been our physician for many years.

Barbara came home from the visit with an appointment for an MRI of her head. My son happened to be home for a few days. The previous day was his birthday. We hadn't mentioned to him what was going on. There was no need to worry him with what we didn't know. Barbara and I thought the worst thing it could be was a minor stroke. We were concerned, but not frightened. Her symptoms hadn't changed since we first noticed them, so we assumed it wasn't getting worse, whatever it was.

His mother and I drove the ten miles to the imaging center. We checked in with the receptionist and waited patiently until her name was called. I sat in the waiting room and pulled a magazine from the pile to read.

A half hour later, Barbara appeared with a nurse at her side. Barbara was her cheery self, but the nurse was all business. With no smile on her face, she said, "Doctor Ed wants to see you both right away."

Something is up. Something serious. Yep, she probably had a stroke.

Barbara and I walked to the parking lot and to our car. We didn't say much. We each knew what the other was thinking. Why did the doctor want to see us so quickly?

Why the urgency? If the nurse had instructed us to make an appointment to see the doctor later in the week we'd know not to worry. I knew from experience that when a doctor wants to see you right after an MRI, it's not because he has good news.

We were both worried as we drove the ten miles to the doctor's office.

When we arrived, I heard a nurse in the back room say, "They're here." Some of the staff behind the desk didn't even look up to greet us, as they would normally have done. They knew something we didn't, and just kept their heads down. Before we could even step up to the receptionist's window, a nurse opened a door and asked us to come with her. She led us to an exam room and told us the doctor would be right in. Barbara and I sat in silence, waiting as if we had just been found guilty in a court of law and were waiting for our sentence to be handed down. We sat there in silence. Barbara was stoic. I reached out and held her hand.

I felt my muscles tense up as soon as I heard the doctor at the door.

He came in, sat down next to us, and said, "You are the last people I'd want to have to tell this to. Barbara you have a brain tumor."

His words went through me like a bolt of lightning. Barbara sat there, expressionless. Tears started to run down my cheeks. I asked the doctor how big the tumor is.

"Six centimeters."

I knew what that meant. It was huge. Mine was four centimeters—about the size of a chicken egg. Hers was the size of an apple.

Barbara sat silently, looking at nothing, her eyebrows pursed with an expression of disbelief. We were so unprepared. We expected that the worst possible news was a mild stroke. Barbara and I had never even considered a second tumor. The odds were too remote. It couldn't happen twice in one household. The hell I had endured with my tumor flashed through my mind.

A few seconds felt like minutes. I was about to ask the doctor what we should do next. Anticipating the words in my mouth, he said to me, "You'd have a better chance of getting her into Lahey Clinic than I would."

My mind raced through the words I had once said to Barbara, *You'll never fully understand what I've been through unless you experience it yourself.* In retrospect, it sounded like a curse, or a challenge. I knew what she didn't know. She was about to find out and it wasn't pleasant.

The doctor continued, "I'll give you some privacy. Take whatever time you need."

And he left the room.

Barbara and sat in silence, numb with disbelief. All I said was, "I love you."

13

On our way home, the silence held. I knew how dangerous a six-centimeter tumor was, but I don't think she quite understood it yet. I kept my fears to myself. She needed support, not more bad news.

When we arrived at home we interrupted Nathan working on school work. We told him what we'd just learned. He was in disbelief. We called our daughter, Amanda, and found her poolside at her apartment in Florida.

"Hi, Amanda."

"What's up, Dad?"

My news was brief and to the point. "Mom has a brain tumor."

First there was uneasy silence. She knew I wouldn't kid about something like that.

Then, choking back tears, she said, "What's going on up there?"

We were all beginning to wonder the same thing.

The next phone call was to Barbara's brother in Western New York. Two brain tumors in one family were beyond comprehension. The reactions from all were the same: "How can that be?" Nonetheless, most people's fears, particularly our children's, were tempered by their previous experience with my brain tumor. Among our friends and family, there seemed to be a feeing that since I survived, so would Barbara.

Barbara had taken time off from work for the MRI. While at home she placed a call to the school secretary to tell her she'd be back at school in a few minutes. Next she contacted one of her friends, one of the Bra-Bras, and asked them to meet her in her office when she arrived. These were her closest friends, her support network. They had all watched with concern as she'd developed a limp, and now they would find out why.

They all gathered in Barbara's office when we arrived, and stood together as Barbara got right to the point.

"I have a brain tumor."

Through the distortion of my tearing eyes, I could see concern, disbelief, and pain on their faces. Seven friends, all in shock. They were speechless. Barbara was holding up well. She might have been thinking that because I had survived a brain tumor she would as well.

I brought Barbara home. How could this be happening a second time? Knowing what is in her future made me feel sick. Just when our lives were beginning to stabilize, a new horror begins to emerge.

It just so happened that my biannual MRI scan was the previous day at Lahey. The worst possible news I thought I could hear was the reoccurrence of a tumor. I had doubts that I'd be able to endure a second battle, so each MRI felt like Russian roulette—following a period of doubt that felt like purgatory. After the first six-month MRI, I broke out in tears in the doctor's office when he announced that all was clear. I had such a pent-up fear that my reaction took me by surprise.

Yesterday, Doctor Carl reviewed the results and had given me the all clear.

The first thing I did at home was to call him back. I told the nurse who I was, and asked if Doctor Carl could see my wife as soon as possible. A nurse at the imaging center gave me a CD of the MRI scans, the pictures of Barbara's brain—we were ready for a consultation. Without trouble, the nurse scheduled us for the next day.

After the workday ended, our driveway filled up with cars—Barbara's friends from school. They all gathered around her in our kitchen, trying to keep the conversation light and positive. Even so, I could hear concern in their voices. The group of friends weren't joking and laughing like they would normally do.

Barbara had always been a central force within this group. She was often the instigator for after school relaxation at the local watering hole, a lady's night out, or a weekend getaway. I could see that they enjoyed her sense of humor, her expertise with computers and her talent with a paint brush. And Barbara loved them all. Right now they were doing what they do so well, supporting Barbara, and supporting each other.

I sat off to the side at the kitchen counter. These friends were vital, and the timing of their presence was perfect. I didn't want to interfere in any way, so I kept my mouth shut. My laptop was on the counter, and being curious, I put the MRI CD in the drive. A few mouse clicks later, the scans of her brain began to appear. Like slices of bread, the MRI built a picture of her brain, slice by slice. In those slices was the essence of Barbara's existence. Everything she thinks and feels and remembers lies within. Her very soul is captured in the neurons now under attack by a cancer.

I started to click through them until I found the tumor. As I went through more slices, the tumor grew and grew. I was shocked. It crowded one side of her brain so that the line between the hemispheres was curved. Fear and panic set in, and I thought I was going to throw up. I slammed the laptop shut, hoping that no one in the room had seen what I had just seen. The tumor was huge, grotesque.

The next day we arrived at Lahey to see Doctor Carl. Barbara and I were shown to an exam room, where we waited nervously for a few minutes before he arrived. I had the CD with me. I didn't want to touch it. The information stored on it repulsed me. I tried to be nonchalant and hide from Barbara how frightened I was by the digital images of the grotesque tumor that was growing in her head.

Doctor Carl walked in and greeted us with a look of curiosity on his face. He said, "What brings you here?"

I offered the CD to him and said, "Take a look at this."

He gingerly took the CD from me by the edges, not wanting to compromise the data side with fingerprints, and he left the room.

Barbara and I sat silently in the room. The same exam room Barbara and I sat in many months before when I was the patient. Being there brought back memories I had of seeing the tumor in my head for the first time. I felt sick then and I felt sick now. We waited until he reappeared a few minutes later. There was no longer a smile on his face. He sat Barbara down and began to examine her neurological functions: Touch your nose with your fingertip, stick your tongue out, etc. I had been through this type of exam many times.

With his flat palm, fingers pointing upward, starting on the side of her head close to her temple, he said, "Tell me when you can see my hand." He began to slowly bring his hand around her head from the left side to check her peripheral vision. It wasn't until his hand was in line with Barbara's nose did she say, "I can see it now."

He didn't react. I didn't either. We both knew what we had both witnessed. On the other hand, to Barbara, everything seemed normal. Her brain hadn't told her that she was almost blind in one eye.

After the examination, Doctor Carl told us the brain tumor needed to be removed. Barbara and I had already discussed the likelihood. We knew more of what to expect this time around, and weren't surprised when Doctor Carl put her on the schedule two weeks out, at the very end of November.

I was now doing the driving. I had learned to compensate for the numbness in my feet and no longer stomped on the pedals. We drove my car back to Southern New Hampshire. Barbara's minivan was being serviced that day and was ready to be picked up. On the way home I asked her if she felt well enough to drive the van back to our house. I'd drop her off and drive my car back. I was a little nervous about it, but it was only two miles and Barbara had been driving just a few days ago without mishap.

We picked up her van at the service station and I drove behind her on the way home. What I saw made me panic. Barbara was driving down the middle of the road and swerving back and forth into the left lane. Driving right behind her, I started to pound on the horn as I waved my arm out the window to get her to pull over. She just kept driving on the left side and wouldn't pull over. As we approached a curve, the first oncoming car had to swerve off the road to avoid a head-on collision. Barbara kept driving. A second car came along and there was another near miss. I kept honking the horn, and she kept driving. My mind raced with mental images of what might happen. I was in full panic mode. Would she make it home alive? Would she injure some innocent motorist? We had only a mile more to go, but would she make it?

With my heart racing, we pulled into our driveway, unharmed. I jumped out of the car and told Barbara that she was driving all over road.

"Why didn't you pull over?" I asked.

She said, "I thought you were just being a jerk." She thought I was criticizing her driving again. In fact I was, but I was also trying to save her life, and possibly someone else's.

A few days passed. The situation was still settling in. Friends stopped by with casseroles, soups, and words of encouragement. The outpouring of love and support was humbling. Everyone wanted to help. Everyone was incredulous.

Barbara's condition deteriorated by the day. Her limp got worse, as did her right-side dexterity. The night before Thanksgiving, we were asleep in bed. In the middle of the night, Barbara nudged me and asked if I would help her make her way to the toilet. Her balance was so poor that she needed help getting out of bed. I came around to her side of the bed where she was now sitting up and helped lift her up off the bed to a standing position. We took one step together toward the bathroom when Barbara's head flopped to the side and her eyes rolled back in her head. Her body went limp and with my arms around her I struggled to hold her upright.

Unable to support her, I lowered her onto the carpet beside the bed. I didn't know what was happening. Had she just fallen asleep, or something worse? For a moment, she lay there making gurgling sounds, like she was snoring. With all my strength I picked her up and maneuvered her back on the bed. What was that all about? I thought about calling 911, but she didn't seem to be in any immediate danger. Once I got her back in bed, she appeared to be sleeping peacefully. I was confused about what I had just witnessed.

I lay down beside her, expecting her to wake up. She didn't, and I eventually fell asleep with my head next to hers and my arm around her. I woke up frequently to check on her. She was breathing okay, and looked peaceful, as if she was enjoying some much-needed sleep. I had never seen a person have a seizure, but I was beginning to believe I had just witnessed one.

That statement I made to her about not being able to completely understand what I had been through played back in my head. She was going to know exactly what I had been through. The thought of knowing what lay ahead for her turned my stomach and weighed heavy on my love for her.

By dawn, we were both awake. Barbara had no recollection of the night's events. Though she appeared to be able to understand my questions, some of her responses were nonsensical. I knew something was wrong. She had changed too much in a day.

From the bedroom phone, I called Doctor Carl's office at Lahey Clinic. After I described what had happened during the night, the nurse told me to bring her to the hospital. I told her I could be there in about an hour.

I helped Barbara get dressed. She was still very wobbly but I managed to walk her down the stairs. She remained in a daze and only spoke when spoken to, and her responses were nonsensical. She was still unsteady on her feet and would have fallen over if unsupported. My son was up and wondering what was happening, but it was obvious to both of us she'd taken a turn for the worse. Because she risked falling down, and we had no wheelchair, Nathan and I placed her in a wooden chair and carried her, chair and all, out the front door and to the front passenger door of the car. We both lifted her into the car. Nathan climbed in the back seat and I drove us to the hospital.

When we arrived, a nurse was waiting at the front door with a wheelchair. Nathan and I lifted Barbara out of the car into the wheelchair. She was lethargic and dazed and said nothing as she was being transported. Nathan accompanied his mom and the nurse while I drove off to find a parking space.

Fifteen minutes later, after circling the parking lot in search of a spot to leave the car, I rode the elevator to the office of Doctor Carl. Nathan was already in the waiting room. Barbara was nowhere in sight, and the nurse explained that she had been admitted to the hospital and was being evaluated. Now was not a convenient time to see her.

The complete reversal of roles continued to sink in. Everything was eerily similar. The doctors were the same. The hospital and even the nurses were the same. The only thing different was that I was no longer the one being pushed around in a wheelchair. It was Barbara's turn. I was no longer the patient, she was.

Our children were faced again with the possibility of losing a parent—but because they had lived this nightmare once before, they were numb to it. Dad survived, and so would Mom. Their anxiety was mitigated by having walked this path once before. I made no attempt to disabuse them of that thought.

Nathan and I left Barbara behind where she would have better care than we could give her. Shortly after arriving home, the phone rang. A nurse from Doctor Carl's office was calling about Barbara. The news was that they had rescheduled the surgery. Instead of the very end of the month, they would operate tomorrow evening.

I didn't ask why, and the nurse didn't offer an explanation.

The reason was obvious.

14

That morning, I made a handful of calls to family members on both sides and close friends. I called our daughter in Florida. We both agreed that now would be a good time for her to come home, so I bought her an airline ticket on the first available flight. She would be home that evening.

Barbara's brother and sister-in-law, Bill and Sue, agreed that the time had come for a visit. They had to have left their house within minutes, because they pulled into our driveway eight hours and five hundred miles later. I picked Amanda up at the airport that evening and we all huddled in the no-longer-empty nest that Barbara and I called home.

Barbara would be on the operating table the following evening. From experience, I knew that this type of surgery might take eight to ten hours. Why would they schedule it to begin late in the day? My head began to circle around that question. It didn't seem like a convenient time for doctors and nurses. Was it the only time they could schedule an operating room? Or was it because Barbara was running out of time?

Quickly enough, we understood.

After a late dinner and somber conversation, we all went to separate bedrooms and fell asleep. At 6 a.m. the phone rang. When it rings so early in the morning, my heart jumps. It might be an announcement that some relative gave birth to a baby overnight, or maybe someone has a broken-down car and needs a ride to work. It's always important. Not knowing what to expect, I grabbed the phone. Everybody else was still in bed.

It was Lahey Clinic calling. "Your wife is in surgery right now." Other words were spoken, but that was all I heard: *surgery right now*.

I hung up the phone and yelled to everyone to wake up. Thoughts were racing through my head. *What happened for them to operate now? It can't be good. Her health must be failing. Is she going to die?*

In no time, I was wide awake. I heard rustling as Nathan, Amanda, Bill and Sue were dressing in their rooms. Preparing to drive the forty miles to the hospital. I wondered what we would find when we arrived. I tried to mentally prepare myself for the worst, but fear over powered me. Had I already seen my wife alive for the last time?

We piled into one vehicle, the minivan that had barely made it home in one piece a few days ago. No one mentioned breakfast or coffee. No one had an appetite, and every one of us was already wide awake.

When we entered the surgeon's office and introduced ourselves, we were told that Barbara was still in surgery, but that's all we were told. At least we knew she was still alive. We all settled uneasily into the waiting room. It was one designated solely for families and friends of people undergoing surgery—the same my family sat in during mine.

I knew it would be a long day. Even though it felt instantaneous from the time I was anesthetized for my surgery to the time I woke up, I was in the operating room for nine hours. Barbara would be in surgery for most of the day, too. To her it would seem like seconds.

Some brain surgeries are performed while the patient is awake. Mine wasn't and I presumed hers wasn't either. For surgery to seem like it lasted seconds and to not be awake to retain the memories was a blessing.

After a while, we ventured out and located the hospital cafeteria. It was bustling with doctors, nurses, patients, and families of patients. While we were enjoying a meal, the love of my life was struggling to live. Guilt settled over me. I looked around the cafeteria and watched people going about their days. All around us in this building people were fighting for their lives. People were dying and babies were being born, but no matter how hard I tried to empathize with the other people, there was only one person in the world who mattered to me at that moment.

A few hours passed and Doctor Carl appeared in the waiting room and sat with us for a moment. Somehow he had found some time to leave the operating room. He said the surgery was going well—as well as can be expected.

He said he removed a piece of tumor the size of his fist. The thought sickened me. He also said he left a section of tumor behind that was about the size of a walnut. Removing it might have caused blindness. Given his meticulousness in removing every last cell of mine, his decision to leave a section of Barbara's tumor in place was extraordinary, but blinding her would have been devastating. I know my wife. She would lose her will to live if she had to go through the rest of her life without seeing.

The section of tumor remaining in her brain would need to be radiated, and she'd have to take chemotherapy drugs. The battle was far from over. Doctor Carl said the tissue he removed looked like an astrocytoma, but the pathology lab would make that determination soon.

The type of tumor is critical to survival. Some tumors, like the ependymoma that was in my head, are survivable. For people with ependymomas, the overall five-year relative survival rate is 81.86 percent. Five-year relative survival rates are highest for those aged 20–44 years (90.8 percent), and decrease with increasing age at diagnosis with a five-year relative survival rate of 61.9 percent for those aged 75 and older.[2]

Because of my own experiences, I had already spent many hours researching brain tumors and knew more than I wanted to know. The five-year relative survival rate for all primary brain and central nervous system tumors is 32.6 percent for males and 35.3 percent for females.[3] Primary brain tumors are tumors that originate in the brain as opposed to those metastasizing from a cancer somewhere else in the body. Roughly a third survive beyond five years. These figures are an average of all brain and central nervous system tumors, but survival rate varies a great deal depending on the tumor type. Some people get a normal lifespan; others die quickly.

---

2 CERN Foundation, Collaborative Ependymoma Research Network
6450 Poe Avenue, Suite 201, Dayton, OH 45414

3 Ibid.

If You Love Me, Take Me Now

It had been only a year and half since I had brain surgery. Now my wife was in the same operating room. I had worried so much about my own mortality. How long would I survive? Where would my life span fall on the bell curve? I worried every day, and now the woman I loved as much as life itself was in trouble. And I still had to be strong for our children. I couldn't even tell them how afraid I was.

Eight hours after the morning phone call, a nurse led us to the recovery room: the same room that Barbara and our children had found me in several months before.

Barbara was lying on her back with wires and tubes connected everywhere. Her head was bandaged and she was still unconscious. With an occasional grunt and groan, she tried to shake off the aesthesia. We were all bewildered, but only I knew how sick she would feel, how much pain she'd be in, and how scared she'd be. I was in the nightmare all over again.

As we gathered around the gurney, Amanda's face became pale and she started to wobble. I caught her as she was about to sink to the floor, and sat her down in a chair. We waited for a long time, sustaining one another by sharing hugs and tears.

Word came from the pathologist that the lab had preliminarily identified the tumor as an oligodendroglioma. Oligodendroglioma is a type of glioma. These develop from a type of glial cell called an oligodendrocyte—the cells that make up the fatty covering of nerve cells. Because they are relatively slow growing, the survival time can be many years. Radiation and chemotherapy are standard treatment after surgery.

At least we now knew what we were dealing with, and I was relieved that it wasn't worse. Even so, Barbara and the rest of the family faced a difficult path.

The next day we drove back to Lahey. Barbara had been moved from the recovery room to intensive care. The nurse said they wanted to keep a close eye on her. We found her asleep in her bed. She looked peaceful as she slept and totally unaware of us being in her room.

The egg-size bump and laceration over her right eye wasn't there the day before, when we saw her in the recovery room. It was obvious, and we would have noticed it yesterday if it had been there then. Her head had struck something hard. When I asked the nurses about what had caused it, all I got was an uneasy silence.

No one would own up to anything. I had no intention of seeking retribution; I was just curious.

My feeling about medical professionals is that they have dedicated their lives to helping others. In that pursuit, nothing is perfect. If an honest mistake is made, I have no desire to sue. On the other hand, if negligence or malfeasance hurts a patient, redress is justified. In this case, I found it hard to believe that someone had deliberately struck Barbara in the forehead. Whatever happened, it was an accident—and sensing the nurses' discomfort, I dropped the subject.

She was hooked up to many wires and tubes. If she made even a small move, it would trigger alarms that summoned help. I remember what that was like: You have to lie on your back all day and all night or you would get tangled in tubes and wires. She had a horseshoe-shaped scar on the right side of her head with dozens of metal staples closing the wound. The nurse told us that she had torn the bandage off the side of her head.

Barbara appeared worse than expected. She was trying to break through the unconsciousness, and managed to open her eyes a crack and mumble a few incoherent words, but then faded away again. She didn't seem to know we were there. Our daughter nearly passed out twice.

The following day, Bill and Sue drove the eight hours back to their home in Western New York. Amanda, Nathan, and I made our way back to the hospital. Barbara now had a bed in a private room. It looked so much like the room I once stayed in that it gave me déjà-vu.

The first person to enter, I recognized immediately. She was a nurse who had taken care of me many months ago. I told her so and she looked at me with doubt in her eyes until I told her what town she lived in and that she is married to a police officer. I couldn't recall her name and I don't think she remembered me; a year had passed, and she had seen plenty of patients since me. Barbara was awake and smiled when she first saw us. She had improved so much. The bandage on the side of her head was new, and as she lay there, she looked happy to see us but tired. Her movements and labored speech proved that she was very weak.

I bent over and gave her a hug and told her I loved her. She reached up to hold me, but with one arm only. After we disengaged, she reached for her right arm with her left hand. She picked up her right arm, released it and let it flop back to the mattress. She could speak, but didn't need words to explain. Her right arm was completely paralyzed. She had absolutely no control over it. Fortunately, her right leg was okay. She said nothing as she tried to hold back tears. Thankfully, though, she could swallow, and wouldn't need a feeding tube.

I learned that she had had a grand mal seizure since surgery. Maybe that contributed to the gash and bump on her forehead; I didn't pursue it.

We stayed as long as we could without wearing Barbara out. My hospital experience had taught me that hosting visitors can be extremely tiring. Visitors were always welcome, but it took extra effort to stay alert and communicative. Sometimes it was impossible to stay awake in their presence.

Doctor Carl stopped by on his rounds to see how his new patient was doing. In a side conversation with me, he commented that Barbara's speech center must be in the other side of her brain, opposite of what is most common. Otherwise, her speech would have been significantly compromised. She had some difficulty, but her ability to pronounce words was not as damaged as it had been in my case. Since Barbara is left-handed, it made sense to me that some of her brain functions would be found on the opposite side.

Here we were, roles reversed. After Doctor Carl left the room, all of us seemed to feel this fact settling in the room. I was able to walk, but only with a cane. My blood pressure would often drop suddenly and I'd have to sit down fast or risk passing out. On several occasions, I was unable to react quickly enough and found myself on the floor. I had bruises and gashes on my head from various episodes. Even though I could sit without risk of passing out, I was nervous about driving a car. But now, Barbara was dealing with her own nightmare. I would never tell her again that she'd never understand—it broke my heart that she did. I knew her pain, her fear, and her exhaustion.

How could this have happened? How could both husband and wife have brain tumors? What was the cause? Was our house toxic? Were we both exposed to a chemical agent? Were our children in danger? We had lived in the same place for decades. Maybe something was in the well water. I had it tested, and found nothing.

Was this nightmare just a horrible coincidence? In a way, that was just as frightening. Either way, I wanted to know the cause.

Barbara spent the next few weeks in the hospital before being transferred to a rehab hospital. Like me, she endured the tubes and wires, the physical pain, the boredom, the anxiety of not knowing how or why.

When I was living on a gurney, her visits were the only thing that made the day pass. Now, I was the one visiting.

I worried that she would not survive. I felt the pressure of providing strong emotional support for our children all the while being a fragile, emotional wreck myself. I knew what it was like for her to take over the extra work of keeping the house and family running; all while balancing myself with a cane, fighting depression, and holding back tears. We were living in a hell like no other.

Barbara was transferred to the same rehab hospital where I had lived for a few weeks. It was closer to home, which meant much less driving for me and for our friends who visited often. Barb rode the ambulance on the same route north on the highway—a trip I had taken only months before. She was retracing my steps every day.

The rehab hospital brought back many bad memories. I remembered the feeding tube in my belly, the suction tube in my mouth, the daily shots in my arm and stomach, the times I had fainted from low blood pressure, my determination to get better and get my life back. Here we were again, but this time it was my lover who was suffering. It tore me apart to know so intimately what she was dealing with.

On a bright note, she was slowly regaining control in her right hand and arm. She could now raise her arm and move her fingers. These improvements gave us hope, something to be happy about.

Steve Cox

Life at home settled into a tense routine. Emotions were fragile, but bottled up—we all knew we were all suffering. My children leaned on me for support and the bond between us grew stronger than ever. My daughter engaged me in conversations that, under normal circumstances, would have been reserved for her mother. Boyfriend issues, female topics that are best dealt with by a mom. Now I was Mom as well as Dad. I even got an occasional hug. My son was maturing in other ways. The realization that he almost lost his dad and the imminent threat of losing his mother shook him out of the bed of security we had raised him in. He was learning that life has no guarantees of happiness or longevity; that it can change in an instant.

15

In early December, I picked Barbara up at the rehab hospital to take her back to Lahey Clinic for an appointment with the tumor board: a team of doctors, nurses, and a social worker who would convene to discuss individual cases and make recommendations. This would be the first time in weeks that we were in contact with the experts.

Even though we found ourselves in a massive snowstorm that day, we didn't want to miss the appointment. We were both eager to learn what they had to say about Barbara's condition and their recommendations for further treatment. We crept along the forty-mile stretch of highway in blizzard conditions. It was a white-knuckle trip that exhausted us before we even arrived.

I wish I could say the meeting erased some of my anxiety. The board confirmed that Barbara's tumor was a high-grade (malignant), fist-sized oligodendroglioma, just as the preliminary report had found. The surgeon once again explained that he had to leave a small pocket of tumor cells in her occipital lobe or risk severe damage.

Barbara would have to undergo radiation treatments and chemotherapy to diminish the remaining bits of tumor and halt the spread of cancer.

The only good news I could take from the meeting was that an oligodendroglioma was treatable and packaged with some hope for long-term survival.

During the meeting, Barbara was oddly jovial, almost as if she were intoxicated. Maybe it was due to her medications or maybe she felt good about being out and about for the first time in a long time.

In a sidebar conversation, the social worker asked, "She doesn't understand how much danger she's in, does she?"

Until that moment, I don't think I had a full understanding, either.

Days turned into weeks, and Barbara was finally doing well enough to come home. She would be released on Christmas Eve. Like me, she was able to walk with a cane, but struggled with it because it required a lot of physical effort. She preferred a wheelchair.

I estimated that she had recovered about 75 percent functionality of her right hand and arm by now. I worried that if she couldn't paint, her creative limitation would be depressing. Both of us suffered from it. The vision in her left eye was still limited, and hadn't improved as much as other functions had. She still couldn't see anyone or anything positioned on her left side. Oddly, this deficit wasn't eminently noticeable to her, but it was very obvious to those around her. Until she realized what the problem was, she often couldn't find the silverware to the left of her dinner plate.

We were the blind leading the blind; the challenged helping the challenged. What a sight. Me with a cane, Barbara in wheelchair. One afternoon I managed to drive us both to the grocery store. It's only about two miles from our house. I pulled into the handicapped spot and wrestled her wheelchair out from the trunk of the car and wheeled her into the store, using the handles of the wheelchair in place of a cane to support myself. My balance was so bad that I'd have to maintain a grip on a handle while I plucked something from a store shelf. I noticed a couple about our age watching us. While we were waiting for our number to be announced at the queue at the deli counter, the gentleman quietly asked, "Car accident?"

I responded, "No, we both had brain tumors."

I'll never forget the look on his face.

Barbara soon started radiation treatments at a hospital nearby, adjuvant with chemotherapy. We didn't want to make daily trips to Lahey Clinic, so I arranged for her treatment to be done at a facility close by. I got approval from the staff at Lahey, and assurances that the local hospital had a good cancer treatment program.

For the next six weeks, Barbara would undergo radiation to her head. During the first visit, the technician custom formed a plastic mask to Barbara's head as she lay on her back on the table. It was necessary to hold her head very still while a focused beam of radiation was sent through her skull into her brain targeting the remaining tumor. The mask would be placed over her face and clamped to the table to prevent her head from moving.

Each day she would need a ride to the hospital and a ride home. Most days, I'd make the ten-mile trek with her and wheel her into the cancer center. While sitting in the waiting room, I'd look around at the other people there and wonder what their situations were. No one talked, but there was a calmness in the room and I felt that we all had unhappy stories.

Barbara's group of friends, the Bra-Bra Sisterhood, stepped in to relieve me of some of the driving. I appreciated the help and was glad to see that being around her friends helped raise her spirits.

February 24 is an anniversary of sorts. Not one I ever plan to celebrate, but that date signifies certain life changing events. It was the day that Barbara received her last dose of radiation, and two years before that, I had had nine hours of brain surgery.

In the hospital there is a ship's bell that sounds when someone has completed their final radiation treatment. It's a ceremonial gesture that the radiation patients (and their spouses) like to hear. Of course, Barbara took her turn at ringing the bell. The hospital staff also gave her a diploma and the mask that held her head still while they used surgical precision to blast the tumor with radiation. It wasn't exactly a memento I wanted to keep, but I kept my opinion to myself when Barbara brought it home.

We were feeling pretty good, in relative terms. We mused that we were fortunate to live near world-class medical facilities. And we were both excited that she has passed this milestone in her treatment. The drive home was no different from any other. We traveled along the country roads lined with snow banks and trees. The wind was blowing, and a few rogue snowflakes snapped at the windshield. Typical New Hampshire weather. I was coming down with a cold or the flu.

When we arrived at home, I went about my business and Barbara pulled out her laptop computer to check her e-mail. She received some bad news from her family. Her aunt had died that morning at dawn. I heard Barb crying in the other room, and she told me the news.

She cried all day. It broke my heart to see her this way. I felt helpless and insignificant. How much more could she endure? What did she do to deserve this? By the end of the day, Barbara's sister-in-law gave Barbara a ticket to fly to Buffalo. It helped console her to know that she could be with her family in a few days.

16

Barb never knew her father. He was General McArthur's Jeep driver in postwar Japan, and spent time in Nagasaki and Hiroshima. A few years later he died of Hodgkin's lymphoma—go figure. Barbara was a year old. She grew up north of Buffalo on Lake Ontario, in the house that her father built before she was born. Her aunt lived next door, and most of the family still lived nearby. Newfane, New York is the quintessential American town. It's a place where you can raise a family and not lock your doors. It's mostly a farming community of down-to-earth people.

The day before her flight I tried to use my frequent flier miles for a ticket, but it was too short of a notice to use them. The best rate I could find was more than we could afford, even though under normal circumstances, you couldn't pay *me* enough to fly to Buffalo in wintertime.

Barbara had an 8 a.m. flight. We didn't sleep well the night before. In between my coughing and her tears, we cuddled in bed talked most of the night. As I held her we reflected on where we were together in our lives. Our empty-nest honeymoon had been interrupted, and we yearned for it to resume. We spoke in terms certain that it would resume. Barbara was never one to give up on a dream. We promised each other that everything was going to turn out OK, and that we would not accept anything less. We believed that we'd have a future, and didn't allow ourselves to think otherwise.

We arrived at the airport that morning for her flight. Feeling as sick as I did, I should have had someone else drive the ten miles. On a good day, I'm dizzy and have poor balance. On this day, it was extreme. I had a hard time driving. The fact that I couldn't feel my right foot didn't help matters, either. But Barb couldn't drive at all. During the ride she was still fighting back tears.

My nephew and his wife were working for a major airline at this airport—the same airline Barbara would be flying with to New York. Anne happened to be working at the check-in counter when we arrived, and checked Barbara in for the flight. From there I pushed Barbara to the elevator and upstairs, through security and to the gate. The people behind us were a little perturbed that it took so long to get Barbara and her wheelchair through security. Anne must have notified her husband, because my nephew, Eric, appeared at the gate to say hi and offer his assistance. Barbara wanted a cup of coffee so I asked

Eric to stay with her while I fetched a cup at a vendor a short stroll from the gate.

I wobbled down the hall with support of my cane to buy some coffee. When I arrived, there was a short line of four or five people in front of me. I stood in line behind what may have been a married couple and patiently waited my turn. In an instant I felt my blood pressure dropping. The "white donut" appeared and blocked most of my vision. It was the warning sign that my blood pressure was dangerously low and I should sit down. Not wanting to lose my place in line, and not seeing a convenient place to sit down, I chose to wait it out. Bad decision. The next thing I knew I had fallen forward on the couple in front of me.

My consciousness quickly stabilized, and I apologized. Seeing my cane, and hearing my slurred speech, I think they accepted the fact that something was wrong with me—that I was disabled. I regained my balance and kept my place in line. Not more than a minute later, the white donut reappeared and I fell forward once again, on the same couple. They grabbed their coffees and departed, mumbling something to one another as they walked away.

Somehow I managed to buy a coffee and make my way back to where Barbara was parked in her wheelchair. I have no recall of the journey between the second time I fell over to when I reached Barbara with coffee in hand. My cane must have known the way back.

When the gate attendant offered pre-boarding for anyone who needed extra assistance, I gave Barbara a kiss and told her I loved her. Eric wheeled her down the ramp and on to the plane. I would spend the next week without seeing Barbara for the first time in months, but I knew she'd be well cared for.

I headed home. Still not feeling well, both physically and emotionally. I don't like to admit it, but I cried the whole way back. I hadn't been this depressed in a long time. I'd be without her for the first time in two years. She wouldn't be at my side, ready to pick me up and dust me off, and likewise me with her.

The next morning, in spite of having had a flu shot, I was struck with a bad case of the flu. I was alone and too sick and too weak to even get out of bed. My balance was so poor that I couldn't make it down a flight of stairs, and had to call a neighbor to help me. That week, I lost ten pounds from an already slim frame, and learned why the flu takes so many lives. It made me worry about mine.

Barbara flew home from Buffalo after spending a week or so with her family. It was not a happy time for her. She was saying goodbye to her aunt and closing that chapter in her life. I drove to the airport that cold winter evening to pick her up. She was already outside waiting for me as I moved the car slowly along the curved road in front of the airport. She was in a wheelchair near the edge of the curb with a dark blanket covering her. Someone had wheeled her there and was kind enough to leave her as comfortable as possible. Standing a few feet behind her was a uniformed police officer keeping an eye on traffic and making sure no one left a car unattended.

When I spotted Barbara I stopped the car right in front of her and stepped out of the driver's seat. She smiled when she saw me walk around the back of the car toward her. The police officer glared at me for a second before he realized that I was there to pick up the lady in the wheelchair. His expression changed to empathy as I pushed her toward the passenger side door. Barbara was still very weak and not able to give me much assistance while maneuvering her from the chair into the car. All the while, I sensed the eyes of the officer upon us.

After I locked Barbara's seatbelt around her I walked back around the car and climbed in behind the wheel. Traffic was very light, but just then the police officer moved to the center of the road and stopped the oncoming cars so that Barbara and I could pull away from the curb. He looked at us sympathetically as we drove past him. His actions weren't necessary, but I could see in his facial expression that he wanted to help in any way he could. That simple act of kindness will always be with me.

It was early March when Barbara had returned from her trip. If anything, it was fortunate that her aunt's death happened after Barb ended radiation treatments. She was able to attend her aunt's funeral and be with family. In retrospect, I should have planned a trip home for her, anyway.

Barb would start chemo again in a few weeks. She could take it at home because it came in pill form. This time she would be taking a much larger dose. Five days on, then a few weeks off. She'd do this for a few months. The side effects would be tolerable—mostly fatigue. She had already lost clumps of hair from her head where the radiation had burned its way into and out of her skull. She had good days and bad, but even the good days often included tears.

Being unemployed and still recovering, I spent all my time at home with Barbara. At home I was able to help her, hold her, and give her the emotional support that I knew first hand was so important. Our love for each other was stronger than ever. Barbara had spent months asking herself how she could comfort me, ease my misery and make me happy. I had such a strong admiration for her. We were both in need and in love.

Our children had resumed their lives and were off on their own. To them, it was just another bad chapter that would eventually have a good ending. Just like when Dad was sick. Their optimism allowed them to step away from their fears and focus on their own lives. Mom and Dad will be OK. Their assumption was no different than mine.

I can't say enough about the support we received from friends and family. Our refrigerator was still filled with casseroles and pies. People were begging for ways to help us, but being who we are, we felt guilty accepting handouts.

Working for the local school system, Barbara's income was a quarter of what it would be if she had the same job in corporate America. My salary had been enough to support the family, so there was no pressure for her to find a higher-paying position. She liked the people she worked with and found satisfaction in what she did. But now her meager salary was barely enough to pay the bills, and the financial pressures began to creep up on us. My long-term disability payments were still in limbo.

The school's human resource manager called us one day to discuss her medical benefits and Barbara's employment status. The next afternoon I drove us to the school's administrative office, which was about five miles from our house. We sat down with the HR manager and learned our fate. By now, Barbara had not been able to work for several months. The way things were going, she'd be out of work for many more. She had used up all her sick time, vacation time, and more. The HR manager had been using every creative way she could think of to keep Barbara on the payroll, but had run out of options. Barbara was being terminated. The school system would no longer send her a paycheck. What was worse is that we would no longer have health insurance.

Barbara and I felt that we were falling through every crack there was in the system. It seemed ludicrous to us that when a person is too sick to work, and when they most need health insurance, those benefits vanished. We felt as if we were being kicked to the curb and then thrown under the bus—victims of a bad system.

The school had tried every legal way to support us. They had known about my brain tumor while Barbara was still working and healthy, and were shocked by Barbara's diagnosis. They offered a last resort, and we took it. They would keep Barbara "in the system" and allow us to pay one hundred percent of the cost of the insurance premiums. That cost was approximately twenty-five thousand dollars per year, paid in monthly installments. It was a lot of money, but less than paying the medical expenses directly. We had no choice. Our savings account began to wither.

Some of Barbara's relatives live in Arizona. One cousin was particularly close with Barbara and asked her to be the matron of honor at her upcoming wedding. Being asked to be in the wedding, and the anticipation of a trip to Arizona, gave Barbara the happiness of something to look forward to. We asked her doctors if it would be okay for her to fly all that way to Arizona and they gave us the go ahead.

Barbara tolerated the chemo well. She'd portion out a week's worth of various medications in a seven-compartment pillbox, one for each day. She had always been the most organized person I had ever met. She'd even make a spreadsheet for grocery items, by store aisle, and print it out before she went shopping. Everything had to be in order, and I didn't mind—it took that burden off of me. But now, each time she sorted pills, she would get very frustrated after a few minutes; even to the point where she would break out in tears. Her mind could no longer handle the coordination that used to come naturally to her. We just assumed it was the chemo. I took over the job of filling her pillbox and organizing it by daily doses.

A month or so after her last dose of radiation, Barbara was scheduled to have a follow-up MRI. It takes that long to determine what effect, if any, the radiation has had on the tumor. They would compare the image of the tumor taken before radiation to the image taken after radiation to see if there had been any changes. We hoped the tumor had shrunk. Our minds had allowed us only the possibility that the tumor was dying, and that our future together was secure. If the tumor had grown, however, the chemo and radiation would have failed. We tried not to think of that possibility.

I was on a biannual MRI schedule; every six months I'd have to "ride the tube." An ependymoma has a recurrence rate significant enough to be a concern—tumors can regrow even after years of remission. I understand how Barbara felt, waiting for her sentence to be handed down by the MRI. I shared her fear. I truly understood.

It just so happened that her follow-up MRI was scheduled for the same day that she was to fly to Arizona. The appointment was in the morning, and not far from the airport, so it would work out well. I would take her to the MRI imaging center and then straight to the airport. Barbara was in good spirits—she had the trip to Arizona to look forward to, and would be seeing her cousins later that afternoon.

The imaging center was in a building about a mile from the hospital where Barbara had received her radiation treatments. We arrived about twenty minutes before her scheduled appointment, checked in, and took a seat next to each other in the waiting room. There were about a half dozen other people ahead of us.

We waited, chatting quietly. She wore a scarf covering her hair and the bald spots on her scalp. I was gazing around the room when she elbowed me to get my attention. She was sitting to my right side on the bench seat up against the wall. When I looked in her direction, she pointed to her chin and I could see that it was trembling. The trembling stopped, she froze in position and had an odd gaze in her eyes.

"Are you okay?" I asked, and got no response.

"Can you speak?"

No response. She just looked through me.

Something was wrong. Her body was rigid. There was a blank stare in her eyes and she couldn't respond to my questions in any way. She needed help, and fast. No one around us seemed to have noticed what was going on. I jumped up and with a few quick steps, leaned through the receptionist's window and said in a low but panicked voice, "My wife is having a seizure."

A few quick steps later I stood in front of Barbara and held her to keep her from falling off the bench. She was still rigid and starting to lean to one side. It was like she was in a trance.

The door on the other side of the reception area burst open and several nurses poured into the room. One of them held Barbara and lowered her to the floor. As she lay there, her breathing became heavy and loud, as if she were winded, and some foam formed on her lips. Two nurses attended to her while the others ushered the other patients out of the waiting room to some other area.

Everything moved in slow motion. This was not what was supposed to happen. We had arrived at the facility in good spirits, thinking the worst was behind us. Barbara would ride the tube and then we'd head for the airport. She'd visit with family and be the matron-of-honor at her cousin's wedding. I just stood and watched, helpless and in shock.

After a few minutes, Barbara began to regain consciousness. An ambulance had been summoned and a gurney was being wheeled into the room from the parking lot outside. Just like that, Barbara was whisked off to the hospital a mile away.

By the time I drove to the hospital and found the emergency room, Barbara was having a CT scan of her head. She was fully conscious and alert when we met up again in a curtained exam space in the emergency area. By now it was clear that she wouldn't be flying to Arizona that afternoon. The only solace was that she hadn't been on a plane when the seizure occurred. Barbara's cousin would have to find a last-minute replacement.

The emergency room doctor told me that the tumor appeared to have shrunk. He was not Barbara's doctor, and we had not met him before that day; he must have been able to access Barbara's medical files. It was the good news we wanted to hear, so I didn't question his findings. I accepted his word as fact, even though in the back of my mind, I felt a bit skeptical.

After an afternoon at the hospital, she was released to my care. We navigated our way to the parking lot—she in a wheelchair, I supporting myself on its handles. We found our car and drove home. The day had been a disaster. Barbara had started it with so much hopeful happiness, and when we arrived at home, she cried. We cried. We sat together and held each other. How could life get worse than it was right now? Our lives were a mess and there was no relief in sight. At least the tumor had shrunk.

17

A few days later, I phoned Barbara's radiation oncologist to reschedule the follow-up MRI. A CT scan taken in an emergency room was not enough for the young doctor; she wanted to compare an MRI to an MRI, not an MRI to a CT. A week later, I brought Barbara back to the imaging center where she'd had the seizure.

We made it through the day without incident and would see the radiation oncologist the following day for the results. We believed we were just going through the motions—that the MRI was a formality.

The car could probably find its own way to the hospital by now. We'd made dozens of round trips. The ten miles due north was mostly back roads, bumpy with ice and potholes. The snow banks on each side of the road were four feet high. The leaves on the trees were still long gone and the wind always seemed to blow, making it feel colder than it actually was.

We arrived at the hospital and waited in an exam room for the doctor. She was an attractive woman who seemed to spend a lot of time in front of a mirror each morning. Her clothes were always impeccable, her hair done professionally and her face had just the right amount of makeup.

Without mincing words she said, "The radiation and chemo didn't work. The tumor has grown."

I was floored. Nauseated. I wanted to think that I hadn't heard her right, but there was no mistaking what she said. It didn't work. The tumor was still growing inside Barbara's head. Everything I had read about oligodendrogliomas said it would work—*should* work. Radiation and chemo were the right treatments.

"What now? What should we do now?" I asked.

Was this the end of the road for treatment? If it was, I knew what the outcome would be. A tumor left growing in one's head always ends in death. I felt panic coming on. By Barbara's reaction I could tell that she didn't comprehend the meaning of it all. The cancer treatment had made her ability to reason a bit fuzzy and she often acted a bit dazed. I knew the meaning, and so did the doctor. I wasn't about to share my fear with Barbara, who was staring expressionless at the doctor.

A million thoughts careened through my head. The doctor dismissed herself from the room. She had done her job, and we were now on our own, with no plan, no direction. I felt abandoned. What should we do now? We drove home in silence.

Barbara had taken care of me when I was incapable of taking care of myself. Without her tenacity, I believe I would not have lived long enough to have surgery. It was now my turn to repay her. To take care of the one who so lovingly kept me alive. At the same time, it made me angry that this monster had tried to kill me, and now it wanted to take the person I loved the most. This disease was monster enough, even, to be the devil's sidekick.

Our children were unaware of everything that was going on with us. I decided they didn't need to know every detail. It would only heighten their anxiety and make their lives more difficult. They knew their mom was sick, but Dad had pulled through and as far as they were concerned so would Mom. They were living their own lives, away from home, and didn't need to be burdened with my fears.

After the short drive home, Barbara went to the bedroom to take a nap. One of the side effects of chemo and radiation is fatigue. Not knowing what to do now, where to go from here, I started making phone calls. This was not the time to give up. Surrendering now would mean certain death for my wife, for the mother of our children. I was determined not to let that happen. We both shared the same neurologist, surgeon, and primary doctors. They all knew of our situation. The common answer I received from them all was to seek out a clinical trial: a controlled study subjecting patients to a course of experimental drugs to test their efficacy. It was our only hope.

All the while, I had been actively communicating with my online ependymoma support group. Their informed advice about navigating the healthcare jungle was priceless. Many of them had had to make critical decisions to save their own lives or the lives of people they were taking care of. Their shared belief was that you need to be your own advocate, or have someone close to you take on that role. No one was going to lead the way for you. You had to find your own path or suffer the consequences—which could be no less than death.

I don't want to speculate what may have become of her if I hadn't taken her to the hospital the morning after her first seizure. Without someone to watch after you, to be a second set of ears during a visit with medical staff, to pick you up when you fall, to fetch and feed you your medicine, you are lost.

My primary care doctor once told me that, "If you just listen to what your patients say, they will often diagnose themselves." If he had not listened to me when I told him that my symptoms were not a "stomach issue," he might have never sent me to a neurologist and I may have not lived long enough to be correctly diagnosed. I lied down next to Barbara and listened to her breathing until I too fell asleep.

The weather was finally turning and giving way to spring. Whenever possible, I'd take Barbara for a ride in the car to help her cope. I'd wheel her through a shopping mall, or once, even a county fair. Otherwise, she was virtually immobile and left with her own thoughts: thoughts of what had happened to us, our family, her husband, and now her.

Meanwhile, I had spoken with doctors at a major cancer center in Boston and made an appointment to bring Barbara there for an evaluation. There were several clinical trials underway, but before making a determination about whether she qualified to participate, they wanted to examine her and her medical records, including the pathology slides made with tumor tissue taken during surgery. The slides were at Lahey, so I made arrangements for them to be delivered to Boston.

Barbara and I made the trek south to the city one sunny morning and followed the directions our GPS squawked at us. We found the hospital near the center of everything and made our way through the security gauntlet into its parking garage. From there we navigated her wheelchair up an elevator and into the waiting room. It was filled with patients and their families. I didn't want to be there. There were no smiles, only very sick people there for their chemo treatments and prognoses. I wondered to myself what the expected remaining time on Earth these people had.

Barbara and I gave our information to the receptionist and I pushed her wheelchair out of the way. There were no empty seats, so I stood balancing myself with a hand on Barbara's chair. Before long, Barbara's name was called and we were led down the hall to an exam room.

The doctor who greeted us was Asian, a professor at Harvard Medical School, and a kind gentleman. He gave Barbara the standard neurological exam while we spoke. I threw in the fact that I myself had survived a brain tumor and watched for his reaction. I hadn't given up the search for a reason why we were both afflicted. I still wanted to know what had brought this evil into our lives.

My disclosure, however, didn't elicit much of a reaction from the doctor. He was focusing on Barbara.

I mentioned that the chemo and radiation had not stopped the oligodendroglioma from growing, and asked him if he knew why. I did expect his answer. Our worst nightmare was about to be cast upon us.

He said, "I examined the slides and the tumor is a glioblastoma multiforme."

"It's not an oligodendroglioma?"

"No."

I was blown away. I already knew what this meant. When I was researching tumors before Barbara became sick, I had read everything I could find about brain tumors of all types. I wanted to know what my chances of survival were. I wanted to find the best course of treatment for me. I had never stopped reading and learning about different tumors and their survival statistics. A glioblastoma multiforme—a.k.a., GBM—was the worst of the worst.

How could it be? How could the lab have made such a mistake? This news was devastating. The oligodendroglioma came packaged with some hope for a cure; the survival statistics were promising. The GBM made the devil look harmless. GBMs are why you get the death look when you tell someone you have a brain tumor.

Barbara was aware that Suzanna, my uncle's wife, had a very dangerous brain tumor, a GBM. I prayed that she had forgotten about it all together. Thankfully, she didn't seem to grasp the meaning. The tumor, chemo, and radiation had taken a toll on Barbara's cognitive skills. She had difficulty doing simple mental tasks like organizing her shopping list and her medications. It was both a curse and a blessing. I would find her in tears when she became frustrated with her limitations. On the other hand, she was blissfully unaware of how much danger she was in.

The treatment for an oligodendroglioma is the same as for a GBM. First there is surgery to debulk or completely remove the tumor, followed by radiation and chemo. In other words, we hadn't lost any time treating the GBM. But because GBMs are the pit bulls of all brain tumors, it now made sense to me why her tumor's growth had not been halted by the chemo and radiation.

I felt sadness and panic all at once. I wasn't going to let her die. I was determined to find every path to a cure. My wife wasn't going to leave me. It just wasn't going to happen.

I felt that the radiation oncologist had given up hope and left us to fend for ourselves. This doctor, however, provided us with several options. And at least there *were* options. He gave me a stack of papers describing three or four clinical trials that Barbara could participate in.

I was a bit surprised that I'd be the one making the decision. It was up to me to choose a path of treatment. Each trial had a different approach. One would test a drug designed to cut off the blood supply to tumor cells, another would attack the tumor directly. It was up to me to make that choice. Fortunately, I had spent my undergraduate years in college studying biology and chemistry, so I had some insight into the individual approaches. I wondered how some other person with no such knowledge could make an intelligent decision. We were told to go home, read the documents, and let him know which one we wanted to pursue.

Barbara's fate was now in my hands.

Looking to give Barbara the greatest chance of survival, I searched the Internet and read every article I could find. I talked with friends in the medical field and contacts I had at the National Institutes of Health. They were all helpful, but none was able to definitively tell me which option was better. I still had to make a choice.

I chose the trial that claimed to produce the fewest side effects. If she was going to be a lab rat for an unproven cure, I wanted foremost for her to survive. Without any ability to predict which trial is more likely to succeed, though, I chose the one that kept her quality of life as high as possible; the one that would alleviate her suffering as much as possible.

We returned to Boston the next week to start the process. I asked the doctor how long Barbara would be in the clinical trial.

He said, "Until we decide it isn't working."

"How much success have you had with this drug?"

Almost gleefully, as if he was reassuring me, he said, "One man lived for a year."

My heart sank. The only consolation was that Barbara wasn't in the room to hear how poor her chances really were.

18

She started receiving intravenous chemo a few days later. We had to make the trek to Boston from New Hampshire for each session. Conveniently for us, there was a branch of this hospital only five miles from our house. Many cancer patients were able to have their chemo administered there, but since this was an experimental drug, it had to be closely monitored in Boston. The local branch, however, saved us the trip to Boston for Barbara's office visits that didn't require a session with a needle in her arm.

We made several trips to Boston for Barbara's experimental chemo treatments. After a short stay in the waiting room with all the other people fighting for their lives, a nurse would appear and call her name. The nurse would lead us down a short hallway to the room where people were being infused with chemicals. One day, as we were following the nurse along the hall toward that room, Barbara stopped walking and reached for me. She leaned back against the wall and started to slide toward the floor. I saw what was happening and eased her the rest of the way down. She was having another seizure. A nurse reacted quickly, called others to help, and took Barbara by wheelchair to a room where she recovered. After a while she was well enough to have another infusion.

The local branch of the Boston-based cancer center was housed in a small wing of a hospital not far from home. The first time we visited, we filled out the obligatory paperwork and signed the legal get-out-of-jail-free release of any legal action against the doctors and hospital. In the waiting room, there was a clear view into the next room where several patients were stretched out on lounge chairs. Beside each was a silver pole from which bags of medicine were hanging—chemo, I assumed. Everyone was considerably older than us, which made me feel a bit odd. Barbara and I were too young to be here.

We met a tall, lanky male doctor about our age. He asked Barbara several questions. Knowing that Barbara may have had some difficulty answering, I blurted out the answers for Barbara. A few glances from the doctor shut me up. I realized he was looking for more than just the answers, such as how Barbara answered them. Did she enunciate clearly? Could she put sentences together? I let him do his work in his own way after that.

His approach was calm and his words were selected with care. He impressed me with his compassion and obvious expertise in working with people fighting life-threatening diseases. All through my own dance with the

Grim Reaper and Barbara's ongoing battle with the devil's sidekick, we were blessed with excellent doctors and nurses, and loving friends and family. As I sat there quietly, relinquishing control, I found one thing to feel grateful about in this nightmarish reality – all of these people truly cared.

We made several trips to Boston for chemo. Despite being glad for the cutting-edge medicine, these trips caused us much anxiety. Before each session a sample of Barbara's blood was drawn and analyzed. If the experimental drug was found to be causing organ damage, she would be removed from the trial. After several weeks of sessions, it was time to take a look at the drug's effect on the tumor. She was to get a new MRI.

After the scan, we waited to see the doctor. He arrived only a few minutes after we were placed in an exam room, and he wasn't smiling.

"The tumor is still growing. We have to take you off the trial."

My mind began to race. What now? This was our last hope!

Barbara's reaction was no different than when we were told that the radiation had no effect on her tumor. She was expressionless. She had relinquished control of her life to me at this point and might have been thinking that I would know what to do next. In fact, I had no idea what to do.

I asked the doctor if there was another trial we could participate in. He said, "Barbara doesn't qualify for any other trial."

I recalled a drug I had read about in my research. It was a promising experimental drug called Avastin. Many doctors had high hopes for it. And one of the ongoing clinical trials here was testing Avastin.

"What about that one?" I asked the doctor.

He said he couldn't get her in the trial, but the drug company might be willing sell Avastin to us directly. The treatment would require two injections per month. The cost was thirty six thousand dollars per injection. Seventy two thousand dollars a month! Not something we could pay for, but we had insurance. There was still hope.

Devastated by the news, we drove home. I hung on to a vestige of hope that our insurance company might pay for the Avastin injections. My hope was abated by the fact that it was an experimental drug. Insurance companies typically did not pay for these. I was going to try anyway—if only to give Barbara hope.

When we arrived at home, I called our insurance provider and was told how to submit the paperwork. I did so that afternoon, and knew the reply might take weeks. Precious time that would allow the tumor in Barbara's head to grow larger.

Meanwhile, it was now mid-summer and Barbara was actually beginning to feel a little better. It had been about eight months since her surgery, and her energy level had improved. She no longer slept for several hours each day, and was more talkative. This might have been because she had not taken chemo of any kind for several weeks. The most egregious side effect of the experimental chemo was fatigue. Even though it failed to work a miracle, I was still glad that I chose the drug for her with mild side effects. For about a week she was even strong enough to get out of her wheelchair and walk with a cane inside the house for short periods of time. Our bedroom is on the second floor of our house and it had been difficult for her to climb the stairs. At the bottom of the stairs, I'd help her out of the wheelchair and half carry her up as she held onto the banister and did her best to put one foot in front of the other until we reached the top.

The letter from the insurance company arrived in late August as the leaves on the trees were beginning to show traces of crimson. It was no surprise that they had turned us down. In the documents they offered a chance to appeal, so I immediately submitted the paperwork. It was a last resort.

A letter came back quickly denying my appeal. Autumn was closing in on us and the change of seasons was in the air.

One day Barbara just sat and cried. When she told me the cause of her tears, I wheeled her to the car and drove her to the emergency room. I had experienced headaches so bad from my brain tumor that I begged for death, and now they were tormenting her. I wasn't going to let her suffer.

When we arrived at the hospital, I headed for the line at the administration desk down the hall—fortunately, it was short today. As we approached the line, some inconsiderate jerk pushed his way around us to get ahead of us in line. I kept my cool and waited the extra few minutes it took to have a doctor see Barbara.

Barbara was given a CT scan and a shot of morphine. The morphine did its magic and we drove home.

A few days later we had one last follow-up visit with the oncologist at the local office of the Boston cancer center.

He had already gone over Barbara's records. After he gave her the standard exam, he set his notebook aside and put his hands in the pockets of his lab coat.

"Why don't you go home and spend time with your family." He glanced at me and I read in his eyes what he had left unspoken.

The bottom fell out of my heart and I wanted to cry. I knew what he was saying. It was the final goodbye. There was nothing else we could do to save her life. The last remnant of hope was whisked from my soul.

The words did not register with Barbara. Her ability to reason and capture nuances had severely deteriorated as the tumor continued to invade her gray matter. She was aware of her mental deficits, though sometimes they worked to ease her depression.

I began to feel helpless. In a way, I wished I hadn't studied brain tumors as much as I had. I knew too well what her chances of survival were. We had exhausted all avenues short of a miracle. Surgery, chemo, radiation, and a clinical trial had not delivered a cure. I felt certain that Barbara would die, and it was time to prepare our children for the inevitable.

19

Our son had come home from college one weekend and our daughter had come to see Mom. One afternoon, while Barbara was napping, the three of us were sitting around the kitchen table. I steered the conversation toward their mother's condition.

"I don't have to tell you that Mom is very sick. Much sicker than we first thought." I hesitated a moment as I struggled with what I had to say next. There was no other way to say it. "Her condition is terminal. She's going to die."

"Don't say that." Amanda was immediately angry.

I had nothing else to say, and neither did they. We sat in silence as the words gathered meaning. One by one we left the kitchen. I wandered into our bedroom and cried. I think our children did the same.

One morning the phone rang. My uncle's wife, Suzanna, had died. There would be a funeral in a few days. The GBM had completed its evil mission.

I hesitated to tell Barbara. She was having some good days, but mostly bad. I'd often find her crying. She knew her health was failing and it was hard for her to cope with it.

I was weakening as well. The veil of strength I had been wearing was beginning to shred. Emotionally, I could not be lower. I could not understand why this was happening to her, me, and to our family. What celestial spirit had I angered and why were we being punished so severely? Physically, I wasn't much different. The numbness on my right side had never subsided, I was still unsteady on my feet, and my speech was far from perfect. But next to Barbara, my tribulations were miniscule.

As a family, we hadn't attended church in a long time. Barbara would often take our children to church when they were young. As they became older, and their friends and children's soccer occupied more of our weekends, going to church lost importance. Knowing Barbara might find comfort re-establishing contact, I asked her if she would like me to take her to church. We started to go every Sunday. I'd drive to the back parking lot of the church where I could easily settle her in her wheel chair. I'd wheel her up the ramp and down the center isle until we found an unoccupied pew. People we know were happy to see us again.

After a few days of conferring with friends and family, they convinced me to tell her about Suzanna.

When I told her she began to cry. She fought her tears and said, "She had the same tumor as I have." For the first time, she seemed to grasp her mortality.

The weight of responsibility was crushing. One side of me continued to search for answers, a cure. The other side was relenting to the realization that the woman I loved so much, the mother of our children, was going to leave us. A day didn't go by without private tears. I still felt I had to be strong for our children. Nathan held his emotions internally and Amanda garnered support from friends and her boyfriend. I sensed both were still holding on to hope that Dad was wrong and Mom was going to get well. I held on to the belief that someone had to be in control while the rest of the world spiraled downward. That someone was me. When I was in a hospital bed trying to survive my own brain tumor, I thought life couldn't get much lower than it was then. I was wrong.

Barbara was no longer able to make her way upstairs, even with my assistance, so I arranged for a hospital bed to be placed in our living room so she could sleep there. It was next to a window and only a dozen steps from a bathroom. Each night I slept on the couch beside her.

A visiting nurse stopped by daily to check on Barbara and give her medications. Our friends and family began to tighten the circle around us. Barbara and I were the epitome of people in need. She was slipping away a little more each day, and I was still struggling with balance and vertigo. Some of the time it still just seemed like a bad dream. How could this be happening? A little more than two years ago, we had been a happy, healthy family of four. I was always in a daze, one foot always in a world of disbelief. My career had vanished, our children were sick with worry, and my wife was going to die. I couldn't imagine how life could get any lower.

On the couch every night next to Barbara's bed, I'd wake up every few hours to give her the medications she needed. In between, I would hear her in fitful sleep and wonder what she was dreaming. I'd listen while she was speaking gibberish and sometimes understand what she was saying. Often, she'd be talking to an old friend. Sometimes she'd wake up and we'd exchange a few words. She'd often start out by asking, "Do you remember the time when you and I ….." After our reminiscing, I'd comfort her and told her I love her, and then we both drifted off to sleep again. This was our lives together, night after night.

In the wee hours of one morning, obviously off in a dream somewhere, I heard her praying to God. She clearly said, "If you love me, take me now."

My broken heart shattered into even smaller pieces.

Every morning, I helped her change her clothes, washed her, and fed her. Her appetite was surprisingly strong and her sense of humor helped us both. Helping her drink from a cupful of medicine one morning, I gave her more than she could swallow in one gulp. She gagged, and coughed and when she was finally able she said, "Are you trying to drown me? What's the hurry?"

To get to the toilet, I'd lower the side rails on the bed, and help her swing her legs around and sit up. After balancing herself for a minute or two, I'd put her in a bear hug and we'd both dance our way to the bathroom. There is one upward step to navigate before entering the hallway where the bathroom is, so using the wheelchair was more trouble than it was worth.

One morning, she had a seizure. As she went limp, I couldn't support her weight and had to lower her to the floor. I made sure she was breathing and then yelled for our daughter. Amanda came running and we both wrestled her back into bed where she regained consciousness in a few minutes. We tried again later and made it without incident to the bathroom and back.

The next morning, the scene repeated itself. Another seizure, and on the second try to maneuver our way to the bathroom, she had another seizure. When the visiting nurse stopped by that day, she inserted a catheter. No more trips the bathroom and no more seizures.

Every day brought more signs that her health was failing. In addition to the physical symptoms, her mind started to drift away. She'd stumble over words, and end sentences without completing a thought. She'd repeat herself and say things that made no sense. She often knew when she was doing this and would apologize and start to cry. She knew she was losing control.

For hours I'd sit next to her bed and we'd talk. The conversation would continue to wander back to our early times together and she'd remember things that we'd hardly ever spoken about. All the way back to the day we first met. During times when she didn't have full consciousness of her condition, she'd even make plans for our future together, a vacation, or a weekend together. She even plotted out a cross country trip she wanted us to take with our kids when summer returned. I'd go along with it, knowing that the tumor was disrupting her thought process.

Other times, she'd have a full grasp on what was happening. With tears in her eyes, she sobbed, "I don't want to die." I felt helpless. I was fighting back tears myself and unable to console her.

Barbara wanted to say goodbye to our children, but they weren't staying at home so she couldn't do it face to face. I bought a small tape recorder so she could use it to leave them a message. A final goodbye from Mom. Words that they could listen to after she was gone. I sat with her and operated the recorder as she spoke to each of them. After a few sentences she'd fall apart and cry too hard to continue. She started a recording by saying, "I want to tell you how much I love you.", and then she'd start to cry.

It became such a painful task that we abandoned it. The memories that I have of her bursting into tears while trying to say goodbye to her children will always haunt me.

Many of Barbara's friends, the Bra-Bras and others, often stopped by the house to offer help. Their visits cheered Barbara up. On more than one occasion, one or two of them would take my place and spend the night on the couch next to Barbara's bed, so that I could catch up on sleep. Amanda had returned to her job in Florida and Nathan had returned to college. The support from the Bra-Bras was all that was holding me together.

Barbara's sister-in-law, Sue, and Cousin Judy arrived from Western New York to help us for a few weeks. Sue and Judy had had always been close to Barbara, and their presence was comforting. It also took some of the burden off my shoulders. Cooking, cleaning, and a compassionate ear helped us get by.

The visiting nurse would often sit down and discuss Barbara's condition with me. She was failing faster and faster each day. Some days she'd sleep through the whole day. I'd have to wake her up to medicate her. Those were the only times when she'd speak. We'd exchange a few sentences and then she'd sleep again. On occasion, she'd be fairly lucid and awake. As much as I resisted the thought, the end was near.

One afternoon the visiting nurse spoke to me about hospice care. The nurse was carefully suggesting that the time had come. My heart resisted the idea, but my head knew it was true. Through my tears, I signed the papers to enter the last chapter of my lover's life. It was a decision I knew was right, but not one I ever anticipated I'd have to make. At least Barbara could remain at our home until the end.

A few days later I received a large envelope in the mail that had US District Court stamped on it. It was a summons. I had been chosen for jury duty. On any normal day I would have been happy to serve. I had often wondered what it would be like to participate in a trial. The timing could not be worse, though, and I thought I might be able to defer because of Barbara's situation.

I called the phone number on the summons. At the other end of the phone was a woman who had obviously heard every excuse in the book. She did not overtly express doubt over my story, but wanted proof. She asked that I send her documentation and the name and number of the hospice organization. I followed her instructions, but a week or so later I received another letter threatening me with arrest for not showing up for jury duty.

After a few nervous phone calls I was able to clear my name. Even so, this event just accentuated the feeling of helplessness I had. No matter how hard I tried to do the right thing, it was for naught. What else was going to go wrong in our lives?

Barbara's sister-in-law had to go back to her life in Western New York. Her husband, Barbara's brother, drove the five hundred miles to pick up his wife and see his sister. It would be the last time he would ever see her. He had to say goodbye to his only sibling for the last time. I left the room to give Barbara and Bill privacy to have their last conversation. It was their final moments together and I didn't want to be in the room. A memory of the scene would have played over and over in my head for the rest of my life, and I was already struggling with too many such memories. We hugged in the driveway before they departed on their long and very painful drive home. Barbara's mother flew in to stay with us a few days later.

I began planning for a funeral. Making arrangements to bury my wife tore me apart. I was full of guilt knowing that I'd be alive and she would not. The only thing I could imagine that could be a more painful experience would be losing a child.

I wanted so badly to find a way to say goodbye. But by doing so I would be telling her I had given up all hope. She was still holding on to hope and I never wanted to discourage that. And besides that, I'm not sure I had the emotional strength to put a string of sentences together without falling apart. We both knew the truth, and we knew each other knew. We left unsaid the word 'goodbye' but we conveyed it in other ways. We spoke about an afterlife, hoping that there was one. She said she'd find a way to give me a signal from the other side.

Over the years of our life together I had gradually garnered the skills to become a serious woodworker. I had actually won a few prizes for making nice furniture. Barbara had always been supportive and helped me find tools and interesting pieces of wood for projects. She was an accomplished crafts person herself. It was a hobby we shared and were passionate about.

Planning her funeral was an emotional process and I had to make a decision about cremation or a casket. Throughout our marriage we had often pondered the what-ifs, so I knew what Barbara's desire was. She would be cremated.

When I allowed myself to believe the end was near, I selected some unique hardwood I had stashed away for a special project. It would become Barbara's burial urn. I applied the best skill I had to shape it into the resting place for my wife's remains. While building it I was filled with conflicting emotions. I had no idea where my life would go from here, but it would be without her. I felt terribly guilty for making plans that did not include her. In an odd sense I felt that by moving on, I'd be abandoning her. It was a beautiful creation, but it pained me to look at it. I took pride in building it, but felt shame that I had not been able to do more for her. It would be the last item I made for her.

When life beats me down I cope by pounding out my thoughts on a keyboard. It helps me organize my thoughts and confront my emotions. Throughout my tumor recovery and Barbara's suffering, I found solace in writing to members of the online brain tumor support group. I had kept them informed throughout the early ordeals of her diagnosis. We were all incredulous that a husband and wife would be stricken with brain tumors, and since then, I'd found that writing to them almost daily was cathartic. They offered practical advice and emotional support.

In happier times, I had joined an online woodworkers group. I wrote the following passage to my woodworking friends.

> *When we were newlyweds, Barbara always encouraged me in my burgeoning hobby of woodworking. When our first child was born, Barbara asked me to make a cradle. My talent was lacking and the cradle showed it, but Barbara loved it because I made it. Today it sits in the back of the attic. Even though it is far from a showpiece, Barbara wouldn't hear of getting rid of it. I honed my skills more with each piece I made and added a kitchen table and a set of chairs. Barbara always had another project lined up for me and every one was an heirloom as far as she was concerned. I moved along from wood butcher to woodworker. She'd buy me tools for Christmas and birthdays. I tried to return the favor with jewelry boxes*

and kitchen cabinets. Almost thirty years later, most of the furniture in the house was made in my shop. Because of Barbara's encouragement and support, those who know me now consider me to be an accomplished woodworker. Last week I made Barbara's burial urn with the tools she provided and the skill she nurtured. Give your wife a big hug today, just because.

The responses I received after posting this message took me by surprise. For me, writing this passage was a way to release some emotions. But it truly touched some people who read it.

Next, I wrote this message to my online brain tumor group.

When Barbara was healthy enough to get around she really enjoyed shopping with friends. I'm convinced there is a shopping gene somewhere on the X chromosome. Barbara called it retail therapy. It gave her so much happiness. Right up until the time that she was losing her cognitive control she thought of shopping. Unfortunately for me, she knew how to shop on the Internet and without a second thought she'd buy things on a whim. She was still planning for the future and would buy art supplies for projects she had planned. She was holding on to the hope that she didn't really have terminal brain cancer. I didn't complain and let her run with it because it made her happy. One day I got a bill for six hundred dollars for some stencils she bought. Geez! It was painful to my wallet, but worth every penny to see how much it kept her spirit alive. I don't know what I'm going to do with all these stencils.

When thinking about our twenty-seven years of marriage, I am so grateful that I told her almost every day that I loved her. There's much truth to the statement that you can't take it with you. I will be able to take with me the knowledge that I did my best to show her how much I appreciated her. I can and will bring that with me to the afterlife.

If I prepare, I can hold my composure. I've been practicing this for two years. It used to be difficult to talk about my brain tumor experience without getting emotional. I'm beyond that now. I can handle what happened to me, but I'm not quite there with Barbara's story. I am really dreading the funeral. I know I'm not going to be strong enough to be strong. It will be the worst day of my life. I feel selfish saying that because it will be even harder for my children and for Barbara's mother.

I try to stay as busy as I can to keep my mind focused on something other than this torturous hell. I'm now both mother and father to my children and have to stay strong for them. Sometimes I get caught off guard and fall apart. The other day I was standing in line at the town hall to get my car registered. I turned around and an old friend was standing right behind me. With her sympathetic greeting I burst into tears right there in front of everyone. She caught me of guard.

Today I did something I never imagined I would be called upon to do. I wrote my wife's eulogy. It took me an hour just to put down the first paragraph. There were too many memories to sort out. It was impossible to say everything I wanted to say. When Barbara passes, someone other than me will have to read it out loud. I just want to wake up and forget this nightmare.

Barbara slept most of the time now. She had stopped eating. Occasionally she'd wake up and say something remarkably lucid and then go back to wherever she was. I bought our daughter a plane ticket to come home. It was time.

Amanda and Barbara's mother helped me with the household chores. I continued to sleep on the couch next to Barbara's bed, half expecting to find her gone when I woke up each morning. A hospice nurse would come by frequently to check on all of us. A minister would drop in and lead us in prayer over Barbara. Days went by.

On the morning of November 6, I was scheduled to have my annual MRI checkup at Lahey Clinic. As always, I was petrified that they might find a new tumor growing in my head. But this time, I was reluctant to make the eighty-mile, round-trip drive not because of what they might find, but because Barbara had not woken up in twenty-four hours and looked particularly pale that morning. Amanda and Barbara's mother were at the house and Nathan had come home from college. The minister was there, too, and I confided my dilemma in him.

He convinced me not to cancel the appointment, saying, "Barbara would want you to go."

After the MRI and the good news from my doctor that all was clear, I drove eighty-five miles per hour on the way home. The neurosurgeon who had operated on both of our tumors had inquired about Barbara; I told him she had only a few days left. I was wrong.

Within an hour of returning from my appointment, Amanda yelled to me, "Dad, something's wrong." From the kitchen I bounded into the other room and looked at Barbara. I knew from what I had read about the end of life that I was seeing it now. Her breathing was labored and the signals were clear.

Amanda was sitting on a stool next to her. In a moment, Nathan and Barbara's mom were in the room with us. It seemed as if Barbara had timed her moment for the most important people in her life to be by her side when she left.

Barbara took her last breath. Tears and sobs broke the room's silence.

I bent over her and kissed her goodbye. As I did so I could hear the soft whisper of air leaving her lungs for the last time as her soul slipped away from her tired body. No longer a mother, a daughter, a sister, a wife. She was gone.

I could hardly breathe.

20

After word had spread, Barbara's closest friends, the Bra-Bras, pulled into the driveway one by one. We all held hands around Barbara's restful body and took turns relating good memories of her being and the grace she had bestowed on our lives.

The next few days were a blur. There was activity around me, but I was numb to it all. It was as if I were watching it all happen from above and through a light fog. I lost track of time.

The funeral happened to be on Veteran's Day. The church was packed with friends and family. There were not enough pews for everyone and many had to remain standing. It was a sunny and warm day for November and the door at the back of the church remained open to the outside. At the park across the street from the church, as the funeral was underway, a Veteran's Day ceremony was unfolding. Quiet reverence to our fallen soldiers was being observed. The drummer in the high school band tapped out a rhythm as the people left the park. Again, Barbara's timing was perfect.

At the cemetery, as a veteran of the US Air Force, she was given full military honors. I was presented with a folded flag by the Honor Guard before taps was played. I could sense that the hundred or so people at her interment were as awestruck as I was by the serenity of her resting place. It was in a very new and small cemetery near the top of a gently sloping hill in an apple orchard. On this beautiful November day, the brilliant sun lit up the golden leaves that still clung to the apple trees.

For the next few weeks nothing was as I expected it to be. Life was supposed to be getting easier, but I found it a little more difficult to cope each day. I'd wake up at 2 a.m. and watch TV. My body ached all over. At some point each day I'd find myself in tears.

Our children were hurting, also. They tried to hide their tears, but I could measure their pain by the tired look in their eyes. I wasn't able to move any of her things. Her toothbrush, deodorant, and bathrobe remained where she had left them. These items were simple but meaningful markers. Reminders of a life of caring and love for one another. I still walked around to the far side of the bed to get in. Her body had given up, but her soul was still alive. I still sensed her presence.

EPILOGUE

After the funeral, Nathan went back to college. Amanda went to stay with Barbara's family for a few months in Western New York, and I found myself alone on a beach in Florida. I don't think we were cognizant of it at the time, but we all had to escape the house and its memories for a while. We were all exhausted, heartbroken, and dazed. What had happened to our family over the past two years was only beginning to sink in. The healing process would take many years and the scars would be on our souls for the rest of our lives.

It has taken me several years to gather enough courage to tell the story. Writing it all down was as much a healing process for me as it may be a sad story for you. It's been a place to release my emotions and dismantle some painful memories. At the least, I hope it is a window into the world of brain cancer.

Too little is known about this disease other than its devastation as it destroys the most critical organ in the human body. Many new drugs and treatments are being tested, but success is still measured in the number of months they add to a patient's life. We need to find treatments that add *years*.

Life for me has changed forever, but I still hold on to much happiness. I have two children, now adults, whom any parent would be proud of. They have each given me grandchildren. Life is good, and would only be better if their grandmother could see them.

Maybe she can.

The brain tumor left me with permanent damage. Compared to what the brain tumor took from Barbara, my issues are trivial. My blood pressure drops dangerously low, often with little warning. I've passed out many times and hit the ground hard. Sometimes I bounce off a wall or television on the way down. My speech is much better, but does become slurred somewhat when I am tired. Full functionality of my tongue never resumed, as evidenced by the loss of ability to whistle. My right side, from head to toe, is numb and tingly. This sensation encompasses half my body. The left side of my throat does not swallow properly. Food and especially pills often get stuck there. My balance is poor and I still get vertigo by looking upward unless I have a hand on something to steady me. I've lost the ability to sneeze and to yawn. There are other things as well, but I'm still alive—and if you met me on the street you'd have difficulty seeing anything out of the ordinary.

The lessons learned from these two years are plentiful, perhaps too many to articulate. One is that the patient is not the only person who is affected by a lesion in their brain. Everyone around them is impacted and some may even need medical attention, albeit a different kind of treatment. Friends and family may suffer from painful emotional wounds. This is especially true for children.

Another lesson I learned is that a seriously ill patient needs to be their own best advocate, or have someone close to them assume that role. The advocate has to be asking questions, taking notes, finding the best care, and demanding attention when they feel they may not be getting all they need. Doctors see many patients and don't always have the time or the singular expertise to manage each patient's health needs exactly the right way each time. If Barbara had not been my advocate, I'm convinced that I wouldn't be here to write this. If I hadn't been hers, her life might have been one year shorter.

I strived all my adult life to become good provider to my family. Success brings with it material possessions. By any standard, we were solidly middle class. A good paycheck and what it can afford are a kind of scorecard of one's success: a nice car, a vacation home, and money in the bank. When lying on my hospital bed, however, these once-important items became valueless. They no longer had any meaning and the pride of owning them vanished.

The adage, "You can't take it with you," is cliché for a good reason. More so, the truly valuable items in life are the things you can't measure or put in your pocket. Good friends, a loving family, a sunny day, a walk in the woods, just being alive are more precious than a nice watch or a sporty car.

If you ever hear someone express the belief that a near-death experience changes one's whole outlook on life, believe them. Believe what they say, because it does. What once might have been an annoyance is now trivial. It takes so much more now to make me angry, and even the smallest pleasures bring me happiness.

I also have a greater empathy for people who face their own challenges and I have a deep respect for nurses. I take immense pleasure in just being able to take a deep breath of fresh air. The simple things in life are the sweetest of them all.

Also by Steve Cox
No Shirt, No Shoes, No Service: A Hitchhiking Memoir

Steve Cox can be contacted at stevec1280@aol.com.

www.ingramcontent.com/pod-product-compliance
Lightning Source LLC
Chambersburg PA
CBHW050533300426
44113CB00012B/2082